ILLUSTRATED WORLD OF NATURE

Adviser: Michael Chinery
Language Consultant: Betty Root

Warwick Press
New York/London/Toronto/Sydney
1987

Published in 1987 by Warwick Press,
387 Park Avenue South, New York, N.Y. 10016.
First published in 1987 by Grisewood
& Dempsey Limited.
Copyright © Grisewood & Dempsey 1984.

6 5 4 3 2 1

Printed in Spain

Library of Congress Catalog Card No. 87-51050
ISBN 0-531-19034-x

Contents

Simple Animals

Animals live in almost every corner of our planet, from the frozen lands near the poles to the deepest parts of the oceans. Animals come in all sizes, from tiny creatures we can only see through a microscope to the great blue whale, the largest of all living animals. Animals, unlike plants, can move about — some fly or swim, others hop or crawl. All animals' bodies are made up of millions of tiny units called cells. (Plants are built of cells too.)

The First Animals

When animals first appeared on earth millions of years ago, they were simple creatures with only one cell which lived in the sea. Very, very slowly, over millions of years, larger and more complicated animals developed.

These early animals had no bones. Animals without bones are called **invertebrates.** Sea creatures such as starfishes, squids, mussels, and lobsters are all invertebrates. So are animals like insects, worms, and spiders which live on land. There are 1,000,000 (one million) or so different kinds or **species** of animal on earth, and all but about 45,000 kinds are invertebrates.

Some invertebrates, such as jellyfishes, depend upon the water they live in to support their soft bodies. Others, such as starfishes, and crabs, are protected by a hard covering over their bodies.

Moving to Land

All animals living on land must protect their bodies from drying out. Some, such as worms and slugs, do this by living in damp places. Other land-living invertebrates called **arthropods** have tough outer coverings to protect them. Their bodies are made in sections and their legs are jointed. Spiders are arthropods and so are insects. Most, but not all, insects have wings. They "breathe" by taking in air through tiny holes in their skin. There are far more insects than any other kind of animal.

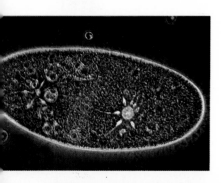

◀ This single-celled animal is shown here 250 times bigger than its actual size. Inside its cell wall is jelly-like material.

▶ Snails' shells protect them from drying out on land; worms and slugs must live in damp places.

▼ Sponges are very simple animals that cling to the rocks. Jellyfishes and sea anemones have soft bodies and stinging tentacles. Corals protect their bodies by building hard cases around them. Starfishes, brittlestars, and sea urchins have spiny skins; other simple animals protect their bodies with hard shells. Squids and cuttlefish developed from shelled creatures.

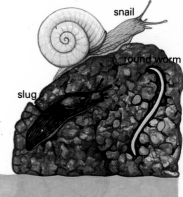

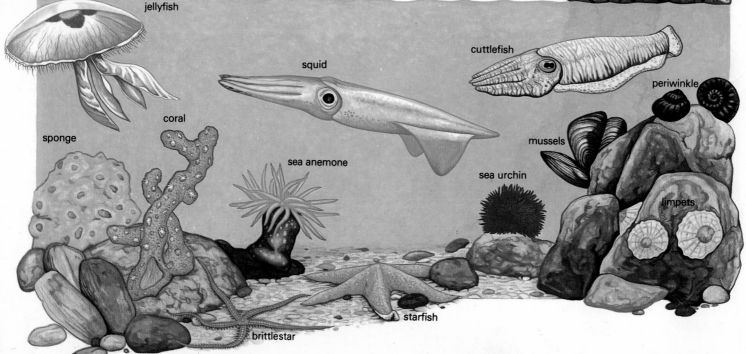

butterfly

hawk moth

bottle fly

hover-fly

spider

damselfly

bumblebee

beetle

ant

centipede

grasshopper

worm

weevil

ladybug

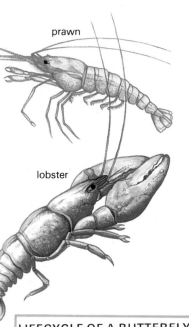

prawn

lobster

▲ The bodies of all these animals are in sections. We call them segmented. Except for the earthworm they are arthropods and have a tough outer covering, jointed to let them move about. They include the many-legged centipede, the eight-legged spider, and the six-legged insects.

◄ Two arthropods that spend their time in water. They are called **crustaceans**. Their bodies are protected by armor-like plates of shell.

PROJECT

WORM STATISTICS

The best way to learn about animals is by looking carefully at them. Here's an easy way to start. First, find an earthworm in your garden or in a nearby park. Hold it lightly by one end and let it dangle. Then measure it; you will be surprised how long it is. Now put it on a piece of paper and listen. As it moves around you will hear quite a loud brushing sound; the worm has bristles on it! Run your fingers gently down it, and you can feel them. Put it back in the earth when you've finished.

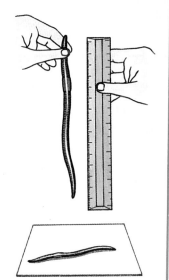

LIFECYCLE OF A BUTTERFLY

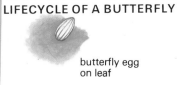

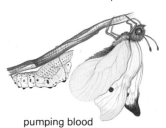

butterfly egg on leaf

caterpillar feeding

caterpillar turns into a pupa

adult butterfly pulls out of pupa

pumping blood into the wings

wings dry and stiff

Fish, Amphibian and Reptiles

The first animal with bones was a small, fish-like creature. It lived nearly 500 million years ago. Animals with backbones are called **vertebrates**, and today thousands of different kinds of vertebrates swim in the sea, crawl, walk, or run on land and fly through the air. Backbones form a framework for an animal's body and allow it to move around easily.

Bony Swimmers

Today there are over 30,000 kinds of fish, living in the sea or in freshwater lakes and ponds, streams, and rivers. Fish breathe through their gills. Tiny blood vessels in the gills take in oxygen from the water. Fish are cold-blooded animals — this means that they do not make their own bodies warm. Instead, their bodies are as hot or cold as their surroundings.

Most female fish lay thousands of eggs into the water. There they are fertilized by the male.

The lungfish can breathe in air as well as in water. It has gills like other fish, but it can also use an air bladder inside its body as a kind of lung to get oxygen from the air.

On to the land

Amphibians are animals that live both on land and in water. Like fish, they are cold-blooded. Frogs, toads, newts, and salamanders are all amphibians. The adults spend much of their time on land, but they lay their eggs in water or in damp places. To start with, the young look more like fish than like their parents. They are called tadpoles and they breathe through gills. Gradually their legs grow, their gills disappear and they get oxygen by breathing air through their mouths into their lungs.

Leathery Eggs

Snakes, turtles and tortoises, lizards, and members of the crocodile family are all **reptiles**. Reptiles' eggs have tough, leathery "shells" which keep them from drying out. This means the eggs can be laid on land. Even turtles that spend all their lives in the sea must come ashore to lay eggs. Some reptiles do not lay eggs, but give birth to babies instead. All reptiles breathe air into lungs. The young look like the adults — they do not go through the different stages that amphibians do.

▲ Sharks and skates have skeletons made of soft bone-like material. This is called **cartilage**. These fish rest on the sea bottom when they are not swimming around.

skate

shark

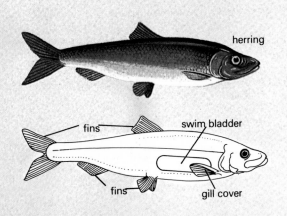

herring

fins

swim bladder

fins

gill cover

▲ Most fish, including the herring, have an air-filled swim bladder which keeps them afloat when they are still. Fins help them move through the water.

plaice

angel fish

eel

▲ Fish come in many different shapes. Flounders are flatfish and they live on the seabed. They are flattened sideways; the upper side, on which both eyes are placed, is spotted for camouflage. Eels are very long and thin. Some of the most colorful fish are the angel fish which can be kept in an aquarium.

Frogs, toads, and newts are all amphibians. They spend their first days in water and then move onto land. They have thin skins which lose moisture easily, so they must keep damp. The pictures below show the life of a frog from an egg, to a tiny water-living tadpole, to a small air-breathing adult.

toad

newt

frog

young frog

tail

tadpoles

eggs

legs

LIFECYCLE OF A FROG

▲ Most reptiles lay eggs with leathery skins. These green-backed turtles are just hatching.

▼ Reptiles include snakes and lizards, tortoises, turtles, and the crocodile family. They are cold-blooded animals and get their warmth from their surroundings. When they are warm they move more quickly than when they are cold; they often lie basking in the sun to warm themselves. They spend cold winters asleep. There are not many kinds of reptiles in countries with cool climates. Most of them live in tropical places.

python

crocodile

crocodile

tic-polonga
(Russell's viper)

frilled lizard

tortoise

Birds

Birds are specially designed to fly. Hollow bones make their bodies light. Their wings and tail feathers allow them to soar, turn, and hover in the air. Most scientists think that birds developed from certain kinds of ancient reptiles. Over millions of years their reptile scales were replaced by feathers, though birds still have scaly legs.

A few birds, such as penguins, ostriches, emus, and kiwis, cannot fly. Others, including ducks, geese, and gulls are good swimmers as well as flyers. All birds have good eyesight, especially hunters such as eagles which spot prey from high in the air.

Birds are among the best known animals, because they are easy to see and hear. Birds move in different ways. Some glide, others hover and some tiny ones dart about.

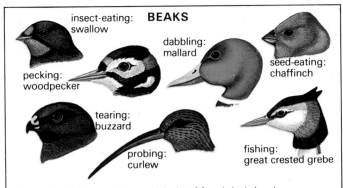

BEAKS

insect-eating: swallow

pecking: woodpecker

dabbling: mallard

seed-eating: chaffinch

tearing: buzzard

probing: curlew

fishing: great crested grebe

Because birds eat different kinds of food their beaks are different shapes. There are strong ones for cracking seeds, long ones for digging, and wide-opening ones for catching insects in flight.

FLIGHTLESS BIRDS

Two birds which cannot fly: the swimming penguin and fast-running ostrich.

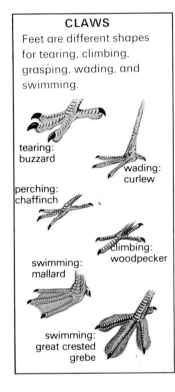

penguin

ostrich

CLAWS

Feet are different shapes for tearing, climbing, grasping, wading, and swimming.

tearing: buzzard

wading: curlew

perching: chaffinch

climbing: woodpecker

swimming: mallard

swimming: great crested grebe

FEATHERS

Birds are the only creatures with a covering of feathers. A small bird like a sparrow has about 2,000, a swan as many as 25,000. The feathers that cover the outside of a bird's body, its wings and its tail are strong and very light. Each feather has a hollow shaft running down the middle. Barbs grow out on either side and lock together with tiny, hooked barbules. Birds spend a lot of time grooming their feathers and keeping them smooth. Under the covering feathers are fluffy down feathers, like those on baby birds. They keep the birds warm.

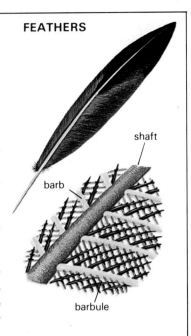

shaft

barb

barbule

We recognize birds by their size and by the coloring and shape of their feathers — their **plumage**. This is not always the same in the same bird. It depends on its age and sex and the time of year. Left: An adult European robin (top) and a young robin. Center: A glossy black male blackbird and its brown female. Right: The black-headed gull in summer (above) and in winter, when its head is nearly white.

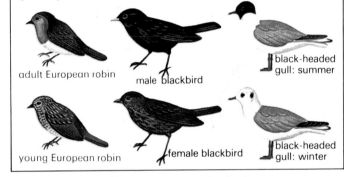

adult European robin

male blackbird

black-headed gull: summer

young European robin

female blackbird

black-headed gull: winter

▼ A stock dove in flight. Its wings are beginning to move up; the feathers are separated to let air through easily. On the down-stroke they are closed to let the wing push strongly downward.

Bird Behavior

Birds spend a good deal of time **preening** — cleaning and arranging their feathers. This keeps their feathers in good condition for flying or for life in the water. Ducks use their beaks to take oil from a special gland on ther backs and spread it over their feathers to make them waterproof.

All birds lay eggs and most birds build nests to lay them in. The young birds are fed and looked after, often by both parents, until they can fly and look after themselves. The male bird chooses an area known as a **territory**. He sings loudly to attract a mate and show other birds where his territory is. He will try to drive off other males of the same species. One or both parents build their nest in the territory, and find most of their family's food there.

Mammals

There are two very important things about mammals. They all have hair, fur, or bristles instead of scales or feathers. All female mammals feed their young with milk from their own bodies. In fact the word "mammal" comes from **mammary glands**, the part of the female's body where milk is made.

Almost all mammals give birth to babies, instead of laying eggs like fish, reptiles, and birds. The early stages of development have taken place in the mother's body. Some mammals are born hairless, blind, and helpless, such as rabbits. Others, such as horses, can move about within minutes of their birth. But all mammal babies are looked after and fed by their parents until they learn to look after themselves.

When they are older, different types of mammals eat different food. Shrews, hedgehogs, and bats eat insects. Rabbits, mice, and guinea pigs gnaw tough food such as bark. Many large mammals such as deer, horses, sheep, cattle, zebras, and giraffes eat grass and leaves. They have hard hooves on their feet. Some have a single hoofed toe on each foot, while others have two toes. We call them cloven-hoofed. Meat and fish eaters such as lions, foxes, seals, and some whales have sharp teeth. Other whales sieve small sea creatures through a fringe in their mouths. Monkeys, apes and people eat many different things. They have sharp teeth for biting, and blunt ones for chewing hard food.

▲ Piglets feeding from their mother. All female mammals make milk to feed their babies.

▼ Many mammals lose their hair twice a year. In winter it may grow thick and long for warmth, and change its color.

roe deer
winter   summer
young deer
rabbit with young

▲ Some mammals, such as the young deer, can move around soon after they are born. But others, among them baby rabbits, are born blind and helpless. They are looked after by their parents and grow very quickly.

▼ Once the world's land was joined in a huge mass. Australia broke away from it early on, and animals there are different from those in other places. One, the duckbilled platypus, lays eggs *and* suckles the young when they hatch! It is called a **monotreme**.

platypus

kangaroo

▲ The kangaroo, less than half an inch long when born, crawls into its mother's pouch to suck her milk. Pouched mammals are called **marsupials**.

There are many different kinds of mammals. We group them together according to how they live and, above all, what they eat.

long-eared bat

insect-eating teeth

shrew

hedgehog

Staying Warm

Mammals, like birds, are warm-blooded animals; they get energy to keep themselves warm from food and oxygen. They have to keep their bodies at an even temperature. Hair or fur helps to keep them warm; sweating or panting helps to cool them down if they get too hot. Sea mammals such as whales and dolphins have thick layers of fat called blubber instead of fur to keep them from losing heat in cold water.

The Cleverest Creatures

Mammals are many sizes, from tiny shrews to large elephants. And they include the most intelligent and successful animals of all — human beings. We belong to the group of mammals called **primates** which includes apes and monkeys. People are intelligent because they have more complicated and better brains than other animals.

monkey

human

gorilla

zebra

single hoof

cloven hoof

gnawing teeth

guinea pig

rabbit

mouse

gazelle

giraffe

lion

fox

meat-eating teeth

dolphin

seal

fish-eating teeth

Animals and People

Animals have always been very important to people. Early people hunted wild animals. They ate their meat, and used their bones to make tools such as needles and fish-hooks. Later on, people learned how to keep animals in flocks and herds. This meant that they could get milk from cows and goats, and wool from sheep. They collected eggs from poultry. Long ago, some large houses had ponds where fish were bred for food. Today fish such as trout are farmed in huge numbers.

For thousand of years, people have trained animals to help them. Several different kinds of animals pull plows and carts, and carry heavy loads. Some can be used to carry people. Dogs help farmers herd their sheep and cattle. They are also trained to help police in many ways, and to guide blind people. Guard dogs will bark when strangers come. All sorts of animals can be trained to hunt, bringing back their catch for food for their owners. Cats are hard to train, but they help people by catching mice and rats.

People also keep animals for pleasure. Some, such as dogs and cats, make good companions. Some are beautiful to look at. But not all animals and people can live well together. Some animals are too wild and dangerous to have as pets in the house. Others harm people by damaging plants and food and spreading dirt and disease.

FOOD

Several animals give us milk.

Butter comes from cows.

Meat comes from farm animals.

Poultry lay eggs.

Poultry and many kinds of fish are good to eat.

Bees make honey.

EVERYDAY OBJECTS

Skins are used for leather.

Furs and skins make clothes and rugs.

Feathers make fans.

Horsehair is used for upholstery.

Wool and silk are woven into materials.

HELP

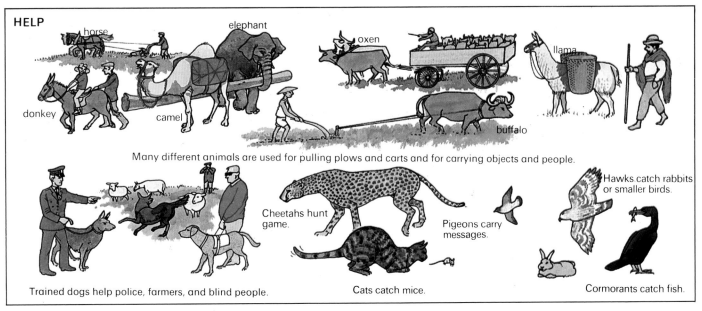

horse, elephant, oxen, llama, donkey, camel, buffalo

Many different animals are used for pulling plows and carts and for carrying objects and people.

Cheetahs hunt game.

Pigeons carry messages.

Hawks catch rabbits or smaller birds.

Trained dogs help police, farmers, and blind people.

Cats catch mice.

Cormorants catch fish.

PLEASURE

fantail pigeon, canaries, dog, parrot, gerbil, hamster, guinea pig, cat, mice, snake, tortoise, terrapin, ornamental ducks

PESTS

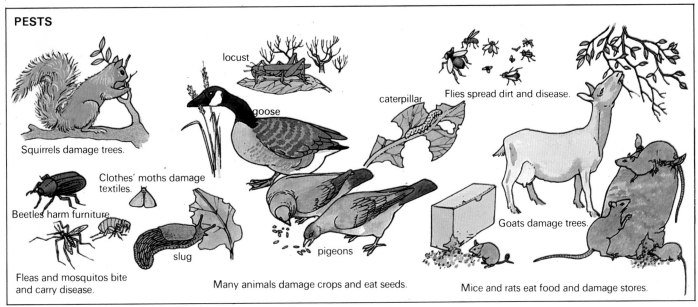

locust, caterpillar, goose

Flies spread dirt and disease.

Squirrels damage trees.

Clothes' moths damage textiles.

Beetles harm furniture.

Goats damage trees.

Fleas and mosquitos bite and carry disease.

slug, pigeons

Many animals damage crops and eat seeds.

Mice and rats eat food and damage stores.

PARTS OF A PLANT

The roots of a plant keep it anchored in the ground. Water and minerals from the soil travel up the roots to the leaves, which contain the chemical **chlorophyll**. This helps the plant make food. The flowers are seed factories. The seeds are scattered onto the ground. In the soil they start growing into new plants.

flower

bud

stem

leaf

leaf stalk

root

(P) This sign is to show you which plants are poisonous. If you see any of these plants, remember DO NOT TOUCH.

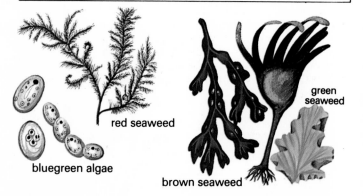

red seaweed

bluegreen algae

brown seaweed

green seaweed

▲ Algae are simple plants. Some of them have only one cell, and float in water or spread over the surface of damp wood. Seaweeds are algae and they are made up of many cells. They have no roots, but they can grip onto rocks. The body of the weed is known as a **thallus**. Some seaweeds are green, some are brown, and some red.

▶ These simple plants have no flowers or seeds. They produce new plants by tiny spores. Most of them are usually found in damp places, although lichens can grow in very dry places.

The Plant Kingdom

What is a plant? Most people agree that it is a living thing made up of a root, a stem, and green leaves. They might add that a plant is unlike an animal because it can make its own food supply, and it cannot move. This is certainly true of most plants — but not of all plants. Seaweeds, for example, have no proper roots, stems, and leaves and are often red or brown in color. Fungi such as mushrooms cannot provide their own food. Some plants are able to move from place to place — but only by floating in water.

The very first plants, like the first animals, appeared in the earth's oceans. They were made up of only one cell. Over millions of years more complicated plants developed, and some began to live on land.

Simple Plants

The smallest plants have only one cell and are called **algae**. They mostly float in water. Together with tiny animals they form plankton, which is eaten by fish and whales. Seaweeds are also algae but are made up of many cells. Seaweeds can be over 130 feet long! Algae use sunlight to make their own food. They all contain the green chemical **chlorophyll**.

horsetail

lichen

lichen

liverwort

moss

mushroom

fern

Molds, mushrooms, and toadstools belong to the group of plants called **fungi** (one of these is a fungus). They cannot make their own food but feed on other things, such as dead leaves. Fungi and algae sometimes live together to form lichens. You can see green, gray, yellow, or orange lichens growing on old buildings, rocks, and trees.

Mosses and liverworts are small green plants that have no proper roots. Instead they have fine threads call **rhizoids**. They have no waterproof coverings, so they usually grow in damp places. Ferns and horse-tails can grow in drier places. Like many other simple plants they spread by producing minute structures called **spores**. Single-celled **bacteria** are grouped with plants. Many break down other living things, causing rot and decay.

Seeds and Flowers

The most complicated plants produce seeds from which new plants will grow. Cone-bearing trees (conifers) have seeds that are partly open to the air. They are attached to a cone, and covered only by scales. The cone-bearing trees are called **gymnosperms** which means "naked seeds." Other plants, called **angiosperms** (which means "seeds in a receptacle") have seeds that are completely enclosed until they are ripe. The peas in a pod are good examples. Angiosperms are the only plants that produce flowers. There are more plants in this group than in any other.

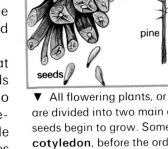

The seeds of gymnosperms are partly uncovered. Trees with cones are gymnosperms. The wooden scales of the pine cone open out in the spring, letting the seeds fly to the ground. Most conifers are evergreens.

▼ All flowering plants, or **angiosperms**, produce seeds. They are divided into two main groups by the way in which their seeds begin to grow. Some produce one seed leaf, or **cotyledon**, before the ordinary leaves. Plants that do this are called **monocotyledons**. They include grasses, bulbs, and palm trees. Others, called **dicotyledons**, produce two seed leaves. These include most flowering trees, and the pea family.

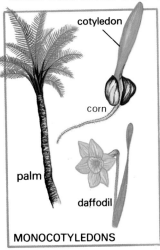

MONOCOTYLEDONS

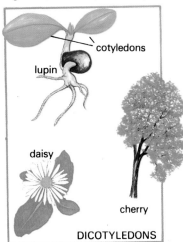

DICOTYLEDONS

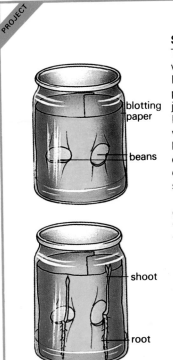

SEE HOW THEY GROW

Take a clean jar and line it with damp blotting paper. Put some beans between the paper and the outside of the jar, as shown in the picture. It does not matter which way you put them. Now keep the jar in a warm place and keep the paper damp. In a few days the seeds will start to grow.

First roots will appear and grow downward (this is always so, whichever way up you put the bean). They take in water. Next a shoot grows upward, and leaves appear on it. Now you can plant your beans in a pot of earth or in the garden, and if you look after them well they will flower and even produce some beans of their own.

HOW PLANTS FEED

The green chemical called chlorophyll in the leaves of plants takes in energy from the sunlight. Water from the soil is sucked up by the plant's roots, and passes through the stem to the leaves. Plants use this water, and the energy from the sunlight, and a gas called carbon dioxide from the air to make the sugar and starch which is their food. At the same time they give out oxygen. We get our food from plants, and from plant-eating animals. We breathe the oxygen the plants give out. Even plants such as fungi which cannot make their own food use the remains of plant and animal life for their food supply.

Trees

A tree is a large plant with a single woody stem. Some trees grow to a huge size: the Californian coast redwood can grow to over 360 feet tall. Trees can also live to a very old age: yews are often over a thousand years old. Trees need a lot of strong roots to hold them firmly in the soil. Their trunks and branches are protected by bark.

There are two main groups of trees. The **gymno-sperms** are the "naked seeded" plants such as conifers. If you look at a fir tree you will notice that its seeds are carried on cones. Its leaves are tough and needle-shaped. Unlike most leaves, these needles do not give out much water into the air. They hold water in, and this makes it possible for conifers to live in very cold or dry climates. Most conifers are **evergreens** — they do not lose their leaves each winter.

The seeds of **angiosperm** trees are normally enclosed in a fruit until they are ripe. Look at the difference between an apple tree and a conifer. The apple tree has broad leaves and scented flowers. The apple seeds (the pips) are surrounded by the juicy fruit. Many broad-leaved trees lose their leaves each winter. They are called **deciduous**. They grow best in a mild climate and stop making food during the winter months. When the warm spring weather comes, the winter buds burst open and new leaves appear. In tropical places, where there is no frost to damage their leaves, broad-leaved trees are ever-green.

A shrub is a plant with several woody stems.

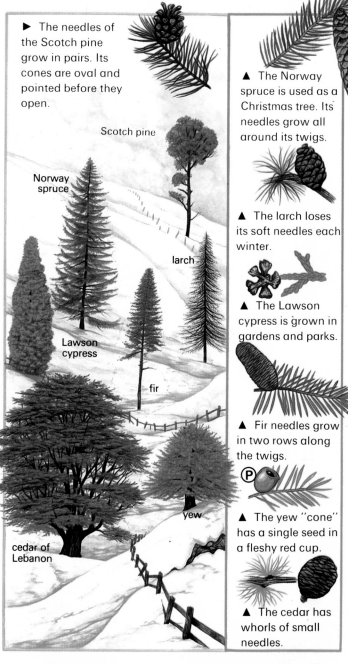

► The needles of the Scotch pine grow in pairs. Its cones are oval and pointed before they open.

Scotch pine

Norway spruce

larch

Lawson cypress

fir

yew

cedar of Lebanon

▲ The Norway spruce is used as a Christmas tree. Its needles grow all around its twigs.

▲ The larch loses its soft needles each winter.

▲ The Lawson cypress is grown in gardens and parks.

▲ Fir needles grow in two rows along the twigs.

Ⓟ

▲ The yew "cone" has a single seed in a fleshy red cup.

▲ The cedar has whorls of small needles.

◄ Most broad-leaved trees shed their leaves in autumn, but the holly is evergreen. It grows as a small tree or shrub (with a number of stems), and is sometimes used as a hedge. The holly's bright red berries provide food for birds and decorations for people at Christmas.

◄ Mixed woodland in autumn. Some of the broad-leaved trees, such as the slender birch, have already lost their leaves. The oak has turned gold and the beech a rich red-brown. Soon their leaves, too, will fall. The dark green pines are evergreens and do not lose their needle-like leaves in winter.

DECIDUOUS TREES

beech

oak

ash

lime

birch

horse chestnut

willow

London plane

---

oak beech ash horse chestnut willow birch

lime London plane

The oak has lobed leaves; its acorns (fruits) grow in shallow cups. Beech trees protect their nuts in spiky husks. The ash has several leaflets on a single stalk; the horse chestnut's leaflets grow from a single point on the stalk. The lime has heartshaped leaves. Willows grow near water; their leaves are long and pointed. The bark of the plane tree peels off; it can grow in cities where the air is dirty. The slender birch has silver-white bark which peels off in strips.

PROJECT

FIND A TREE'S AGE

5ft.

growth rings

How old is a tree? A rough-and-ready way to find out is to measure its girth (the distance around its trunk). This works best on large trees standing by themselves. Trees with close neighbors grow more slowly than normal.

Take a piece of string and measure around the tree about 5 feet from the ground. Every inch of girth shows about one year's growth.

If you find a tree stump, you can tell the age at which the tree was cut down by counting the growth rings. Each ring stands for one year's growth.

TREES IN BLOOM

Broad-leaved trees belong to the **angiosperms**, or flowering plants. Most of their flowers are small and not very noticeable, but some have colorful and strong-smelling flowers. The hawthorn, elder, and wild cherry all grow wild; others shown here are grown in gardens or orchards.

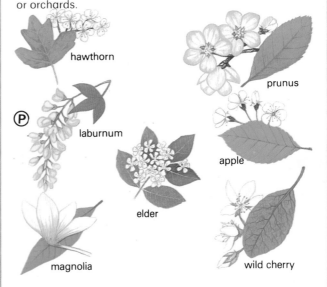

hawthorn

prunus

Ⓟ

laburnum

apple

elder

magnolia

wild cherry

17

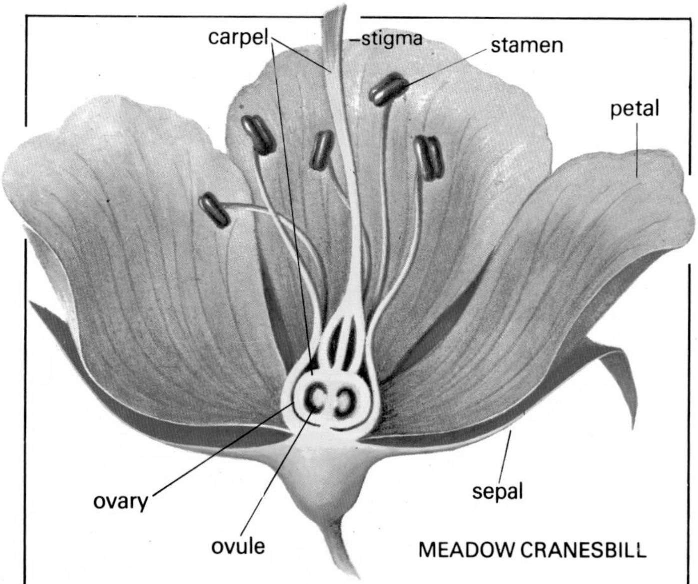
carpel
stigma
stamen
petal
ovary
sepal
ovule
MEADOW CRANESBILL

The different parts of a flower. The **stamen** is the male part, which produces pollen. The female part is the **carpel**, which includes the **ovary**. The pollen grows down to the **ovule** (egg) to make seeds. The **sepals** are small leaves which protect the flower when it is in bud.

▼ One of the best ways of recognizing flowers and telling which family they come from is by their petals. The poppy has four petals, all alike; the rose has five. Some of the vetch's petals are shaped differently from others. The harebell's petals are joined in a bell. The daisy is made up of dozens of tiny flowers packed tightly in one head; the hogweed has many flowers on short stems.

Flowering Plants

When we look at flowers, we notice how pretty they are, or how sweetly they smell. We often forget that each flower is there for a purpose. Flowers have to make seeds, from which new plants can grow. They do their job very well; there are more flowering plants in the world than any other kind. They come in many shapes and sizes. On one pond you may find a wild water lily flower, 6 inches across, growing next to a duckweed flower so tiny that you need a microscope to see it.

The Parts of a Flower

Never pick rare flowers, or uproot any wild flowers. Instead, pick a single common flower such as a buttercup, and see how it is made. The diagram on the left shows the parts of a flower. Seeds cannot be made until pollen from a male part reaches the female part. This is called **pollination**. The shapes and colors of flowers, and the way in which they grow, are related to the way in which they are pollinated.

▼ Another way of recognizing flowers and their families is by the way in which their flowers and leaves are arranged on the stem. Some grow singly, others in rows or clusters. Some flowering plants grow upright, but others grow in low clusters or creep along the ground.

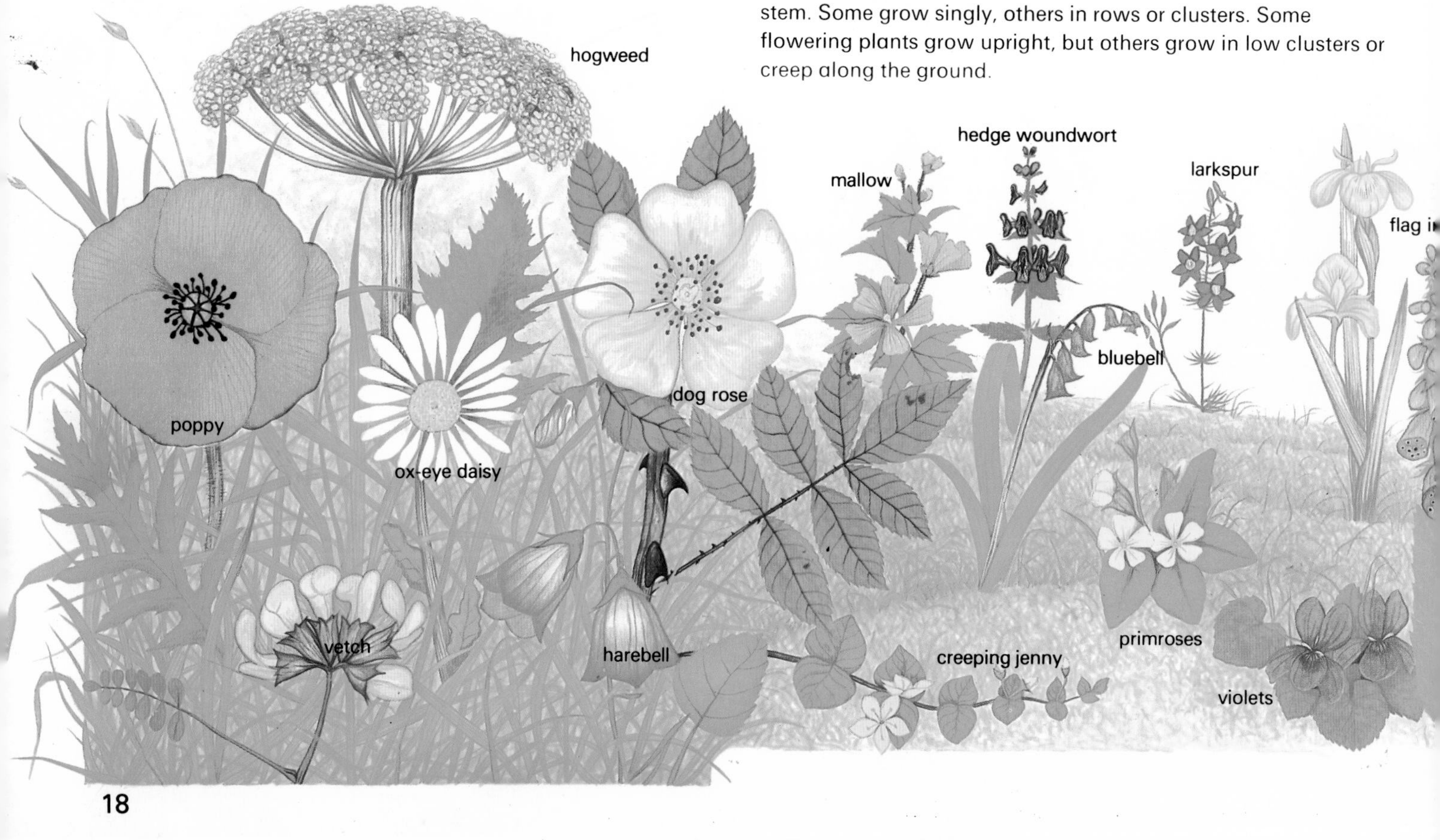
hogweed
hedge woundwort
mallow
larkspur
flag i
bluebell
dog rose
poppy
ox-eye daisy
vetch
harebell
creeping jenny
primroses
violets

Some flowers can make seeds when their own pollen reaches their ovule. But most flowers need the pollen from a different flower of the same kind. This pollen is sometimes carried by the wind. Other plants rely on insects. Their flowers make a sugary liquid called nectar, which the insects love to drink. The colors and smell of their flowers are specially designed to attract insects and lead them to the nectar. As the insects are feeding, the pollen is rubbed off on their bodies. Then they carry it to the next flower they visit.

Flowering plants are grouped together according to the shape of their petals and the way in which they grow. Look at them closely to see the differences. What color are the petals? Is each one the same size? What shape are they, and how many are there on each flower? Is there one flower on each stem, or are there lots of little ones? Look too at the shapes of their leaves and how they are arranged on the stem.

Some plants, such as the poppy, live for only a few months. They are called **annuals. Biennials** begin to grow from seed one year, and flower and die the next. The foxglove is one of these. Many plants live for a number of years. They are called **perennials**. Many of them die down each autumn and come up again in spring. They use food stored in roots or underground stems. Trees and shrubs are perennials.

▼ These garden plants are larger, brighter relatives of wild ones opposite. Here are the pairs: angelica — hogweed; hollyhock — mallow; delphinium — larkspur; *Stachys* — woundwort; aster — daisy; campanula — harebell; pansy — violet; sweet pea — vetch. Foxglove and primroses grow wild and in gardens.

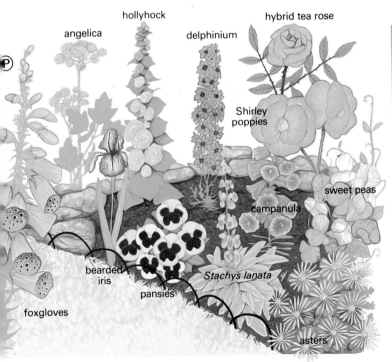

angelica • hollyhock • delphinium • hybrid tea rose • Shirley poppies • sweet peas • campanula • bearded iris • Stachys lanata • pansies • foxgloves • asters

pitcher plant

The leaves of the North American pitcher plant (above) form a jug or pitcher. Insects in search of nectar fall in and are eaten. The sundew (below) also traps insects. Their juices make up for the lack of food in poor soil.

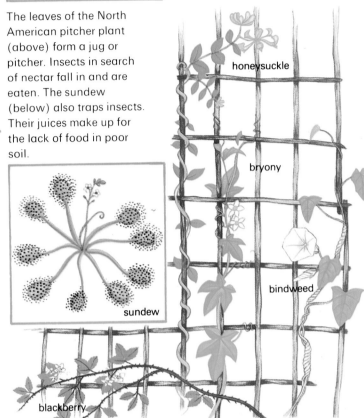
sundew • honeysuckle • bryony • bindweed • blackberry

▼ Climbing plants. Some plants are supported by a strong woody stem. But others twist around other plants, or climb fences or walls. Bryony has little spiral shoots which grip. These are known as **tendrils**. The blackberry grips with its thorny stem.

PROJECT

PRESSING FLOWERS

Make a wildflower collection by pressing them, mounting them in a book, and writing down just where and when you found them. Only pick common flowers like daisies and buttercups, and **never** dig up the plant.

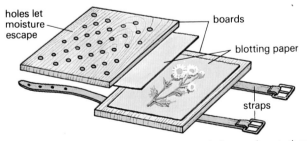
holes let moisture escape • boards • blotting paper • straps

Make sure the flowers are clean and dry and put them carefully between two sheets of blotting paper. You can make a flower press from two pieces of plywood or hardboard and two straps. Put the flowers and blotting paper between the boards and strap them tightly together. The flowers should be quite dry in two weeks.

POLLINATION

Flowering plants reproduce by making seeds. To do this, a pollen cell from the male part of the flower must meet the ovule of a female part. The wind blows pollen to the female part in catkins and grasses. Insects and birds help other plants by carrying pollen from flower to flower in their search for nectar.

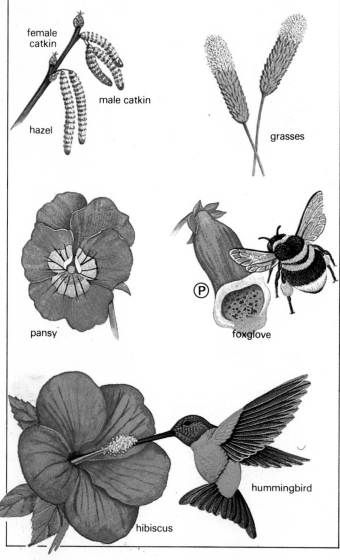

female catkin

male catkin

hazel

grasses

pansy

(P)

foxglove

hibiscus

hummingbird

Most plants have quite short lives. The must produce new plants to take their place when they die. They do this in many different ways. Plants that have only one cell often just split into two separate cells. Toadstools and mushrooms scatter spores from under their caps at the rate of 100 million an hour. Some of them will form new growth. Ferns carry spores on the underside of their leaves.

Most plants have seeds. They are produced when a pollen cell from male parts meets the ovule or egg of the female part. Conifers have male and female cones. The male cones produce pollen. The wind blows this on to the female cones. On page 18 we described how flowering plants are pollinated.

A Place to Grow

Producing seeds for new plants is not the end of the story. They must find a good place in which to grow. If seeds simply fell to the ground beneath the parent plant there would not be room for them all to grow. So all sorts of ways of spreading seeds to new places have developed. This is known as **seed dispersal**. Some of the ways of spreading seeds are shown on the next page. They are so successful that just a few years after a new island is formed from a volcano under the sea, it is covered with plants whose seeds have been brought by water, wind, and animals.

Many flowering plants can spread in other ways too. Trees send up new shoots from their roots. Blackberry stems make new roots when their tips touch the ground. You can cut or break off shoots from geraniums. If you plant them in damp soil, they soon grow their own roots and make new plants.

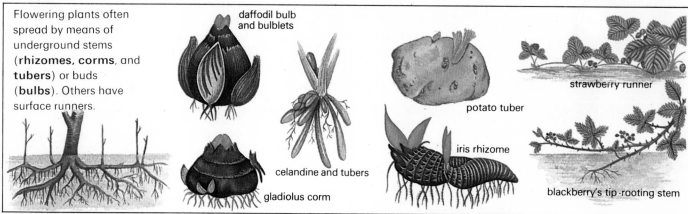

Flowering plants often spread by means of underground stems (**rhizomes, corms**, and **tubers**) or buds (**bulbs**). Others have surface runners.

daffodil bulb and bulblets

strawberry runner

potato tuber

celandine and tubers

gladiolus corm

iris rhizome

blackberry's tip-rooting stem

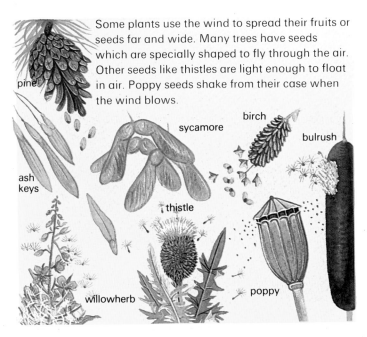

Some plants use the wind to spread their fruits or seeds far and wide. Many trees have seeds which are specially shaped to fly through the air. Other seeds like thistles are light enough to float in air. Poppy seeds shake from their case when the wind blows.

pine

ash keys

sycamore

birch

bulrush

thistle

poppy

willowherb

▲ A dormouse likes to eat blackberries. Many plants have seed coverings that are good to eat, so they attract animals and birds.

wood avens

goosegrass

agrimony

burr

Some plants use humans or animals to spread their seeds. Spiky seedcases and flowerheads (called burrs) cling to fur and cloth, and drop to the ground away from the parent plant. Goosegrass (cleavers) is covered in tiny hooks that will stick to almost anything.

laburnum ℗

coconut

The seeds of the laburnum tree grow in long pods. When these are dry they split and twist apart, shooting out the seeds.

Some seeds are scattered by water. The coconut is often washed from one tropical shore to another, where it grows.

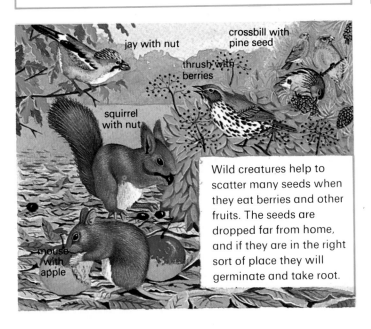

jay with nut

crossbill with pine seed

thrush with berries

squirrel with nut

mouse with apple

Wild creatures help to scatter many seeds when they eat berries and other fruits. The seeds are dropped far from home, and if they are in the right sort of place they will germinate and take root.

PROJECT

WATCH THEM GROW

Some seeds grow in an amazingly short time. Buy a packet of cress seeds. Put a piece of damp flannel or blotting paper in a shallow dish, and sow the seeds on top of it. It is fun to make the first letter of your name.

After only a few days the seeds will start to grow, and in 12 to 15 days the cress will be ready to eat.

Take a leaf from an African violet or a begonia, and make cuts through some of the veins. Again put the leaf on moist soil, and first roots and then a new plant will grow.

cress

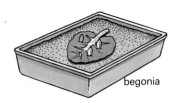

begonia

Plants We Use

Without plants, there would be no people and no animals in the world. We all need plants in order to live. The very first human beings used to eat berries and fruits which they found growing wild. They also hunted plant-eating animals. There are still people in the world today who live in this way. About ten thousand years ago, however, the first farms started to appear. People started to keep animals which could provide them with food. They began to grow wild plants as well. This is called **cultivation**. Over the ages, farmers picked out and bred only the very best plants.

Today we still rely on plants for our food. Wheat, barley, oats, rye, rice, and corn are the most important crops. They are known as **cereals**. Vegetables and fruits keep us healthy. Herbs and spices make our food tasty. Sugar is a sweetener: it comes both from the tropical sugarcane plant, and from the root of the sugar beet. Olives, sunflower seeds, and groundnuts are among the many seeds and fruits which give us oils when they are pressed. Some fungi can be eaten, too — but some are very poisonous. Seeds, fruits, and leaves are used to make drinks.

Many wild plants are useful as medicines. The dried leaves of the foxglove are used to make digitalis — a medicine used for heart complaints. Trees provide us with timber for building and paper-making. Rubber is made from latex — the juice of the rubber tree. Even though people can make artificial fibers (such as polyester), we still use plants such as cotton to make cloth. Plants supply dyes and scents.

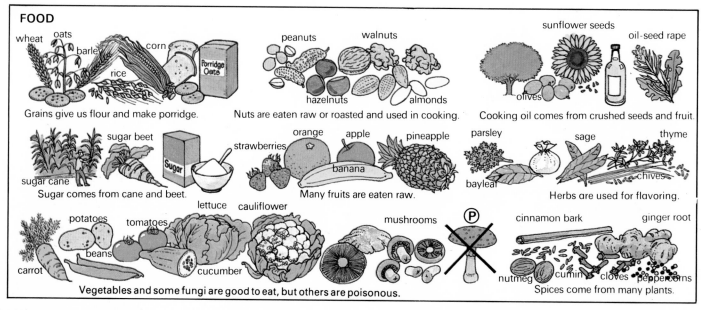

FOOD

wheat / oats / barley / corn / rice / Porridge Oats
Grains give us flour and make porridge.

peanuts / walnuts / hazelnuts / almonds
Nuts are eaten raw or roasted and used in cooking.

sunflower seeds / oil-seed rape / olives
Cooking oil comes from crushed seeds and fruit.

sugar beet / sugar cane / Sugar
Sugar comes from cane and beet.

strawberries / orange / apple / pineapple / banana
Many fruits are eaten raw.

parsley / sage / thyme / bayleaf / chives
Herbs are used for flavoring.

carrot / potatoes / tomatoes / beans / lettuce / cauliflower / cucumber / mushrooms ℗
Vegetables and some fungi are good to eat, but others are poisonous.

cinnamon bark / ginger root / nutmeg / cumin / cloves / peppercorns
Spices come from many plants.

DRINKS

barley / hops
Hops and barley make beer

Grapes make grapejuice and wine.

Apples make cider.

orange / blackcurrants / lemons
Many fruits make drinks and syrups.

coffee beans / coffee / tea leaves / tea / cacao
Cacao beans make chocolate.

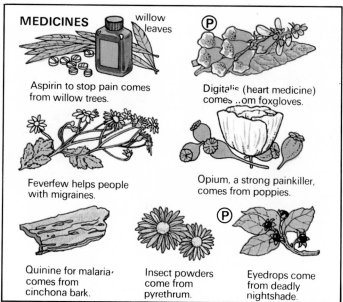

MEDICINES

willow leaves
Aspirin to stop pain comes from willow trees.

℗
Digitalis (heart medicine) comes from foxgloves.

Feverfew helps people with migraines.

Opium, a strong painkiller, comes from poppies.

Quinine for malaria comes from cinchona bark.

Insect powders come from pyrethrum.

℗
Eyedrops come from deadly nightshade.

PRODUCTS FROM TREES

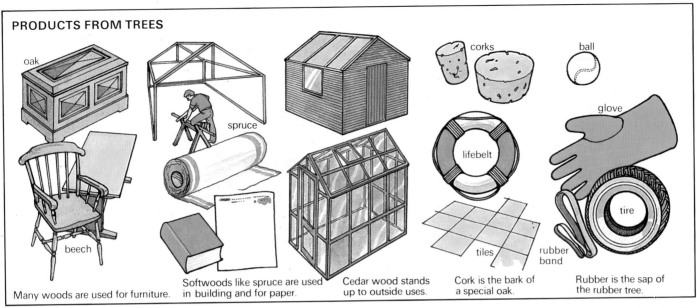

oak

corks

ball

spruce

glove

lifebelt

tire

tiles

rubber band

beech

Many woods are used for furniture.

Softwoods like spruce are used in building and for paper.

Cedar wood stands up to outside uses.

Cork is the bark of a special oak.

Rubber is the sap of the rubber tree.

FIBERS

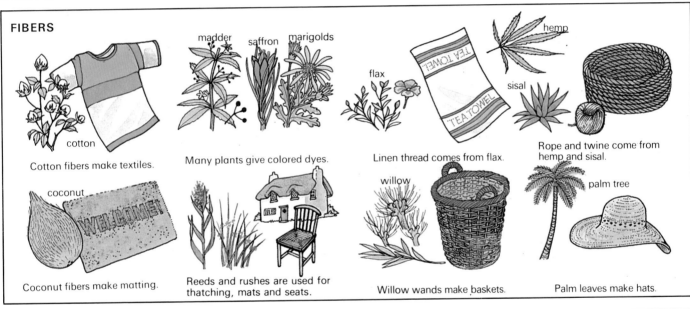

madder

saffron

marigolds

hemp

flax

sisal

cotton

Cotton fibers make textiles.

Many plants give colored dyes.

Linen thread comes from flax.

Rope and twine come from hemp and sisal.

coconut

willow

palm tree

Coconut fibers make matting.

Reeds and rushes are used for thatching, mats and seats.

Willow wands make baskets.

Palm leaves make hats.

PLEASURE

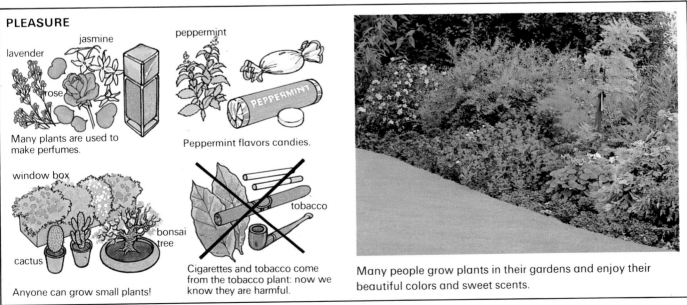

jasmine

peppermint

lavender

rose

Many plants are used to make perfumes.

Peppermint flavors candies.

window box

tobacco

bonsai tree

cactus

Anyone can grow small plants!

Cigarettes and tobacco come from the tobacco plant: now we know they are harmful.

Many people grow plants in their gardens and enjoy their beautiful colors and sweet scents.

thistle
bindweed
kestrel
seagulls
jackdaws
swallow
swallows
house martins
plane tree
cat
weeds
coot
sequoia
cedar
Leban
lime
rabbits
pigeons
dog
squirrels
bulrushes
mallard
stickleback
swan
perch
moorhen

Towns, Gardens, and Parks

▲ This picture shows how towns and parks provide plenty of places for wildlife to live in.

A **habitat** is the place where an animal lives or a plant grows. A town may not seem a good habitat. But if you look around you will find all sorts of things living there. Begin with your own home, where there are certain to be lots of insects, spiders, and perhaps unwanted creatures such as woodworm and mice. Many birds like towns. A few, including pigeons, starlings, and sparrows, live in the busiest parts, nesting on buildings and feeding on scraps. You may even see seagulls, house martins, swallows, and swifts in towns and cities. But most birds such as tits, robins, thrushes, and blackbirds prefer to live where there are gardens and parks with bushes, trees, seeds, and insects. Where there is a lake or river you may see waterbirds such as moorhens, ducks, and swans, and in the lake there will be fish and water creatures such as the ones described on page 34. Other creatures which live in gardens include squirrels, perhaps a few rabbits, and even sometimes a fox, which finds food in garbage cans. A town garden can grow all sorts of flowers, but there are many other plants which grow wild in towns. Dandelions, bindweed, willowherb, and other wild flowers can be found on building sites, railroad embankments and any open spaces.

Wildlife in the Garden

If you live in a house with a garden, you can try to attract wild creatures to live there. First, make sure it will be a good place for them. Is the garden big enough? Will they be safe from cats, dogs, and children running around?

An easy way to attract animals is to put out food for them. We tell you how to feed birds on the right. You can encourage birds — particularly tits and sparrows — to build a nest in your garden by putting up a nesting box. Fix it to a wall or a tree, but do not put it in full sunlight as the heat inside could kill the baby birds.

A good way to attract wildlife is to plant the sort of shrubs and flowers which they particularly like. Hollyhocks are favorites with bees, and buddleia with butterflies. Shrubs with berries provide food for birds in late autumn and winter. If there is room, allow one corner of the garden to stay wild, with small bushes, brambles, and nettles growing untidily there. They make a good home for insects, shy birds, and small mammals.

▼ Even a small house and garden contain a great many different kinds of animals and plants. Some trees and plants are particularly good for attracting insects and birds, and a pond has all sorts of tiny creatures living in it.

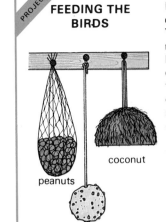

PROJECT

FEEDING THE BIRDS

Birds will visit your garden every day if you put out food for them. You can put it on a bird table, but remember that this must be at least 6 feet high so that cats cannot jump on it. Pet shops sell food for wild birds, and you can also put out household scraps such as bread, bacon rind, cheese, and suet. Hang up a net of peanuts — but make sure that they are not salted, as salt is bad for birds. Hang out half a coconut. When the shell is empty, fill it with a "pudding" made of seeds and scraps stuck together with melted fat. When it is cold and solid, hang that out too. Once you begin to feed birds in winter you **must** keep it up regularly; they will rely on your food and may not be strong enough to look elsewhere.

Hedgerows and Fields

Our countrside is a patchwork of fields divided by hedgerows. These are a mixture of large bushes such as elder, hawthorn, blackthorn, and hazel with straggling brambles, tall grasses, nettles, and all kinds of wild flowers. Their leaves, seeds and berries provide food for insects, birds and small mammals. Thick hedges can give shelter too to all these creatures. Birds like finches, dunnocks, warblers, and wrens all feed and nest there, while the tangled undergrowth hides voles, mice, toads, spiders, and even adders.

Meadow life

Grassy meadows can be as crowded with life as hedgerows. Among the grasses grow all kinds of flowers — daisies, buttercups, dandelions, and clovers. They attract bees and butterflies looking for nectar. Grasshoppers, caterpillars, snails, and slugs eat leaves and stems, while underground there are worms, moles, ants, and beetles. Larger animals such as rabbits and deer come to feed at dawn and dusk. On chalky hills, you can find orchids in the short grass and all through the year the gorse has yellow flowers.

Farm fields used for growing crops or grazing animals have far fewer kinds of wildlife. Chemical weed killers destroy most wild flowers, although poppies often survive and shoot up among the corn. As the fields are so wide and open, there is little cover for animal life. A few creatures, such as moles, live underground; others, such as hares, rely on speed to escape from enemies. Some birds, such as lapwings and skylarks, nest on the ground; often their eggs are stone-colored for camouflage.

hawthorn

wren

black-headed gull

spider

oil-seed rape

cow parsley

yellowhammer

maple

nettles

cows

lapwings

red campion

buttercups

ragwort

hare

daisies

cinnabar moth

mole

field vole

woodmouse

speedwell

weasel

clover

The picture opposite shows hedges and meadows in May. Birds and insects are busy with their young. Caterpillars hatch out from butterfly eggs and feed on leaves; lapwings search the ground for grubs to give to their chicks. In the distance, gulls follow the tractor looking for food in the plowed-up soil. In another field grows brilliant yellow oilseed rape.

Below is downland in July. Butterflies flutter over the low-growing flowers and a skylark rises singing over the grazing sheep. A field of golden wheat in the distance is nearly ready to harvest.

MOUNTING A SPIDERWEB

You can often find a spiderweb in a hedge. The best way to study it is to mount it on a piece of card. To do this you will need a piece of black card, some glue, and some talcum powder in a spray. You will also need patience, because this takes a lot of care!

Find the most perfect web you can, and make sure the spider isn't on it. Spray it lightly with the talcum powder until it looks white. Cover the card with a thin layer of glue. Now bring the card up very gently behind the web until they are touching. Snap the threads that hold the web to the hedge — and lift it away.

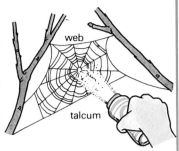

web

talcum

glue-covered card

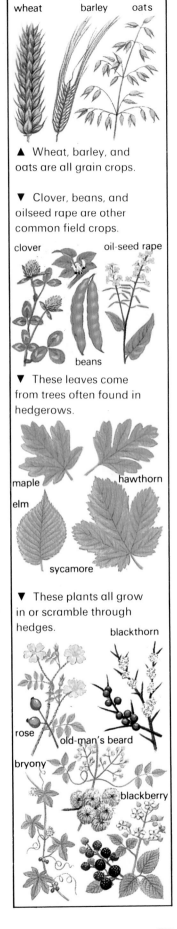

wheat   barley   oats

▲ Wheat, barley, and oats are all grain crops.

▼ Clover, beans, and oilseed rape are other common field crops.

clover   oil-seed rape

beans

▼ These leaves come from trees often found in hedgerows.

maple   hawthorn

elm

sycamore

▼ These plants all grow in or scramble through hedges.

blackthorn

rose   old-man's beard

bryony

blackberry

skylark

oak

wheat

salad burnet

gorse

sheep

grass

grasshopper

dog rose

bee orchid

lizard

common blue butterfly

small copper butterfly

thyme

lesser spotted
woodpecker

marsh
tit

birch

hazel

squirrel

bluebells

oak

muntjac

badger

roe deer

red
campion

bracken

oxslips

hedgehog

wood anemones

woodmouse

violets

bank vole

Woodlands

There are three main types of woodland in the world: coniferous, deciduous, and rainforest which is found in tropical places (see page 56).

Deciduous trees, such as ash, beech, elm, and oak shed their leaves in autumn. In early spring, the sun shines through the bare branches, so that all kinds of plants — shrubs, ferns, flowers, mosses, and lichens — begin to grow. With such a variety of plant life, deciduous woodlands are home for many birds and small mammals. Some feed on the seeds and fruits of plants and trees; others eat insects and grubs.

Coniferous trees have cones and, except for the larch, are all evergreen. This means they do not lose their needle leaves in winter. Because the trees are always covered in leaves, little or no sunlight gets through. This makes coniferous woods dark, shady places. Plants cannot grow without light, so there are few flowers or bushes beneath the trees. Instead, the ground is thick with old, fallen needles.

Various insects live in the bark of conifers and these are eaten by insect-eating birds like the tree creeper. Other birds found among conifers include the crossbill, which has a special scissor beak for tearing open cones, and some birds of prey, especially owls. Deer and red squirrels are both quite common in these forests.

magpie

jay

crossbill

long-eared owl

tree creeper

red deer

spruce

rosebay willow herb

fox

pine marten

stoat

red squirrel

foxgloves

wood ant's nest

weasel

pine

bedstraw

fly agarics

lady's tresses

shrew

On the left of the picture is an oak wood, in the center a wood of mixed trees, and on the right a coniferous forest. You can see the sorts of plants that grow in the different kinds of wood and the animals that live there. In the clearing in the middle are animals that are found near the edge of all kinds of woodland.

BARK AND LEAF PRINTS

When you go for a walk in the woods, take with you some thin, strong paper, some string or a few thumbtacks and a wax crayon. With these you can make bark rubbings. Tie or pin a piece of paper to a tree trunk. (Be careful not to damage it at all.) Now rub the paper firmly with the crayon until a pattern appears. You will find that each kind of tree has its own special pattern.

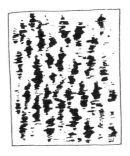

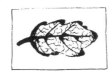

Make leaf prints by painting the back of a leaf with thick poster paint (don't make it too wet.) Put the leaf, paint side down, on a sheet of clean paper. Now put another sheet of paper on top, and press it down firmly with your hand or with a rolling pin. This will give you a print of all the veins in the leaf. You can use spray paint too, or even shoe polish, but these can be a bit messy; if you do use them, spread plenty of newspaper around.

Moorlands and Mountains

Moorlands and mountains are high, cold, and windy places. Even so, all but the highest mountains have their own plant and animal life.

As the ground rises, the air temperature drops, making it hard for plants to grow. Trees, especially, cannot live in very cold conditions. The point on the mountainside where tree growth stops is called the tree line. Below the tree line, conifers and birches are common species. Rowans grow alongside streams. Plants above the tree line lie low on the ground, often in the shelter of rocks, to escape the bitter wind. Dry heathlands above the tree line are covered with lichen, heather, grass, and shrubs such as bilberry. Wet moorland plants include sphagnum moss, rushes, and cotton grass. Wet moorland soil is very poor and two plants — the sundew and butterwort — add to their food supply by catching and digesting insects.

▲ In winter the mountain hare changes its coat to white. This acts as camouflage against the snow. The ptarmigan also has a special white plumage for winter. This disguise makes it harder for enemies, like eagles and foxes, to see it.

conifers

birches

red grouse

ring ouzel

heather

red deer

curlews

saxifrage

purple moor grass

greenshank

bilberries

stream

grass of Parnassus

adder

butterwort

sphagnum moss

Highland Animals

Many upland birds are summer visitors only. In winter, curlews, greenshanks, snow buntings, ring ouzels, plovers, and dotterels all fly down to warmer valleys and seashores. Only red grouse and ptarmigan live in the highlands all year round. The red grouse feeds on heather shoots and the seeds and berries of low-growing shrubs; higher up, above the tree line, the ptarmigan scratches the bare, rocky ground for seeds and insects.

Overhead, golden eagles soar, watching the ground below. They have extremely good eyesight and can spot prey — hares, grouse, and ptarmigan — from a distance of a mile. Ravens, members of the crow family, also fly high in the sky ready to drop down and scavenge.

Frogs and newts can be found on wet moors and snakes in drier heathlands. Herds of deer are common, mostly in summer.

▼ Thousands of years ago, people cut down trees and burned away bushes to clear land for cattle and sheep. Over the centuries, the grazing animals destroyed most of the plant life in these areas, leaving treeless areas of moor and heath like the one below. The mountain rocks (right) are above the tree line.

golden eagle

alpine gentian

ravens

dotterel

mountain hare

mountain ash (rowan)

cliffs

creeping willow

ptarmigan

golden plovers

cotton grass

snow bunting (summer)

snow buntings (winter)

ndew

Spring, Summer...

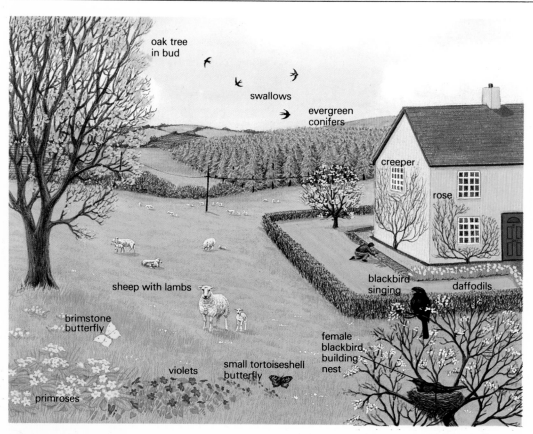

oak tree
in bud

swallows

evergreen
conifers

creeper

rose

blackbird
singing

daffodils

sheep with lambs

brimstone
butterfly

female
blackbird
building
nest

violets

small tortoiseshell
butterfly

primroses

◄ In spring, the days get warmer and stay light for a longer time. Primroses, violets, daffodils, and other early flowers come into bloom, while on the trees leaf buds burst open. Dormice wake up from their long winter sleep and butterflies come out of winter hiding places. Some animals already have young: foxes and badgers look after their babies in the shelter of underground burrows, but sheep rear lambs in the open fields. Many birds have already mated; while the female blackbird sits on the nest, the male sings loudly, warning other birds to keep away. More and more insects breed and insect-eating birds, such as swallows, fly back from winter homes in warmer countries.

trees in
full leaf

swallows

creeper

rose

summer flowers

deer with
fawn

buttercups

old-man's
beard

fox and cubs

hawthorn

peacock
butterfly

young blue tits

red admiral
butterfly

clover

dandelions

bramble

◄ In summer all this activity begins to slow down. Leaves cover the trees while meadows and gardens are colorful with flowers. About this time, evergreen trees shed some of their old leaves, but all trees are producing food — some for growth and some for storing until next year. Insects are everywhere, breeding quickly in the long, warm summer days; honey bees collect honey and store it away for the winter. Birds are too busy looking after their young to sing so much. By mid-summer, some of them are rearing their second or third family. Large animals, like deer, have their young in summer when there is plenty of fresh grass. If the summer is dry, worms curl up in the soil and wait until rain makes it damp enough for them to come out again.

Autumn, and Winter

▶ In autumn, days get cooler and shorter and animals and plants must prepare for the coming winter. Insects are few so many insect-eating birds fly away to warmer lands. Swallows collect together on overhead wires before setting off for the south. But chaffinches, which feed on insects during the summer, now change their diet to seeds. Many small mammals are busy eating fruits and nuts to give them extra fat for winter warmth. Squirrels bury nuts for future use — but often forget where they are. Bats and dormice get ready to sleep through the cold weather (**hibernate**). Because the days are cool the air is damp and this means that fungi can grow up and scatter their spores.

▶ During the cold days of winter, plants stop growing and rest. The large, flat leaves of deciduous trees and hedges have fallen off, but the tough, waxy leaves of evergreen trees stay on. Because evergreen trees keep their leaves, the ground beneath stays almost clear of frost and snow. Here birds and mammals can scratch around for food. Many animals shed their summer coats and grow a thicker, warmer one for winter. In northern areas, the stoat puts on a white winter coat which acts as camouflage against the snow. Redwings, fieldfares, geese, and other birds from cold lands farther north arrive looking for food. When snow covers the ground, look for the tracks made by different creatures.

Freshwater Life

More than half the earth's surface is covered with water. Most of this is the salt water of seas and oceans. Inland, rivers, ponds, and most lakes contain fresh water. Many plants and creatures make their homes in fresh water, but few of these can also survive in the sea, because of the salt. The kind of life that develops in fresh water depends on how much oxygen there is. At the bottom of a pond or canal where the water does not move there is very little oxygen. In a fast-moving stream there is a lot. Rain washes minerals from the soil into fresh water, which help plants grow.

Ponds and Lakes

Most freshwater habitats are full of life. Even a large puddle in a field will soon fill up with algae, tiny insects, and water fleas. In a pond these creatures are eaten by fish such as the three-spined stickleback, by water beetles, and by amphibians such as the newt. Gnats and dragonflies can be seen flying over the pond. Some insects actually walk on the top of the

◀ As a river flows to the sea it goes through many changes. It may start off bubbling through peat and tumbling over rocks. The river bed may change to sand or gravel. Later, the river may wind slowly through marshes or meadows. Near the sea the tide slows up the river and it becomes salty. Different creatures live in different parts of the river. The salmon lives part of its life in the sea, but it journeys up the whole length of the river in order to breed. When the young salmon are big enough they swim downstream to the sea, but they will return to the very same river to lay their own eggs.

▼ The still water of a pond is a home to many creatures. Insects breed here, and so do fish, crustaceans, mollusks, water spiders and amphibians. In spring you can often see tadpoles, hatching out from frog spawn.

RIVER

waterfall

stonefly young

bullhead

wagtail

dipper

FAST STREAM

caddis fly young

mayfly

young salmon

brown trout

noctule bat

heron

alders

kingfisher

willow

SLOW RIVER

reeds

perch

water vole

sand martin

TIDAL WATERS

elvers

iris

salmon

eel

otter

marsh marigolds

POND

toad

pond skater

snail

frog

tadpole

stickleback

newt

ram's horn snail

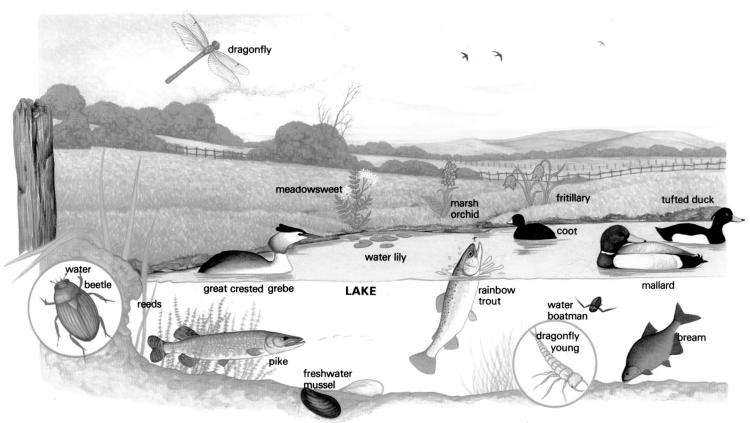

dragonfly

meadowsweet

marsh orchid

fritillary

tufted duck

coot

water lily

water beetle

reeds

great crested grebe

LAKE

rainbow trout

water boatman

dragonfly young

mallard

bream

pike

freshwater mussel

water. On the bottom of the pond are young insects: these often look very different from the adult insects. Hiding among the pond weeds are tiny water snails. Every animal in the pond feeds on another creature or plant living there.

Large lakes may have rather bigger creatures living in them. Big fish such as the pike can easily gulp down a water vole or even a diving bird. Lakes may also be the home of large birds such as swans. Mountain lakes sometimes have fewer plants and animals.

Streams and Rivers

Many of the creatures to be found in ponds or lakes are also found in rivers. However, some wildlife is found only along the river. When a river springs up it is often only a tiny stream. As it winds through the countryside it is joined by other streams and becomes a river. Soon it widens, and finally opens out into the sea. Different creatures and plants are found at each stage of the river's journey. The dipper likes fast streams. It ducks into the water to pick insects off the bottom. The kingfisher digs a tunnel in the river bank

▶ Pond dipping is a fascinating hobby. Spring and summer are the best times, when the pond is full of small animals. You will need a net and some jars or plastic boxes. A magnifying glass is very useful too. When you have looked at an animal, return it to the water quickly. It is best to go pond dipping with a grown-up in case you fall in.

▲ A shallow lowland lake. Freshwater mussels filter food from the rich water. Large fish are to be found here, and there is space enough for all kinds of water fowl. The reeds and other plants around the lake make a hiding place and a nesting site for the birds.

and then makes a nest at the end of it. If you are very lucky you may find an otter on the river bank.

Pollution is spoiling many of our rivers and freshwater lakes. The water is being poisoned, sometimes by the waste from factories, sometimes by garbage and sewage. Often farmers use chemicals on their crops. Rain washes these into the water, where they kill wildlife. When pollution is stopped, the wildlife returns.

A SHELL COLLECTION

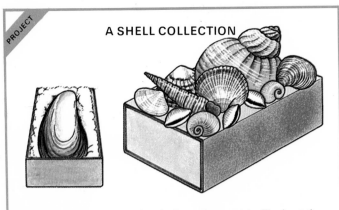

It is fascinating to look for shells at the seaside. The best time to find them is at low tide when most of the beach is uncovered. Do take a grown-up with you, and keep an eye on the tide so that you are not cut off when the sea comes in again. On a sandy shore you can find empty shells along the high tide line. If you are looking among rocks, wear an old pair of shoes. Leave live shellfish where you find them, and collect only the empty shells.

Wash the shells when you get home, and brush them with a soft brush. Dry them carefully. Keep the best ones in the bottom of a large matchbox lined with cotton and covered with cling-film. Put a label on the front, saying where you found the shells and what kind they are. Any extra shells can be stuck as decoration on matchboxes, which make good presents. First cover the top and bottom of the box with plain-colored paper.

The Seashore

Between the land and the sea is the shore. There is always plenty of wildlife here. The waves of the sea are very powerful. As they strike the land, they turn soil into mud and grind stones and shells into a fine sand. Some rocks are broken down into shingle and pebbles. Other rocks are very hard and wear down very slowly. Different plants and animals are to be found on each type of shore, but they all have one thing in common. They must be able to live on land and in the sea, because twice a day the shore is covered by the tide.

The plants of the shore must be tough. Where the water does not reach, you find grasses and other flowering plants such as marram and sea holly. These need tough leaves because of the salty spray, and strong roots to hold them firm in gales. Clumps of thrift cling to cliff ledges and lichens spread over rock faces. The beach itself is the home of many algae. On the upper part of the beach or rocks you will find

▼ The seashore is rich in animal and plant life. This attracts all kinds of birds searching for food. Oystercatchers are wading birds, which can be seen strutting along the water's edge. They use their long red beaks to probe the mud. Despite their name, their favorite foods are cockles and mussels. The herring gull and the black-headed gull will eat almost anything they can find on the seashore.

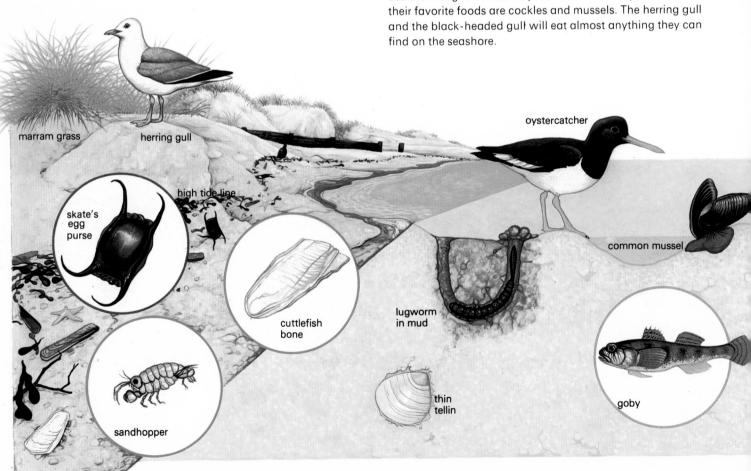

marram grass

herring gull

oystercatcher

high tide line

skate's egg purse

cuttlefish bone

common mussel

lugworm in mud

sandhopper

thin tellin

goby

green seaweeds. Farther down are brown and then red seaweeds.

You can usually see a line of seaweeds and rubbish which shows you the high tide mark. This is a good place to find empty shells, dead shore creatures such as crabs, and "mermaid's purses" — the egg cases of sharks and rays.

The areas below the high tide mark is the home of all kinds of animals, including many burrowing worms. Among the sand and seaweed you will find **mollusks**. The **bivalves** — such as tellins, mussels, and razor shells — have a shell which is hinged in two parts. Many of these lie buried in the sand, and others are attached to rocks. They filter their food from the seawater as it comes in. The "snail" type of mollusk, such as the whelk and periwinkle, is called a **gastropod**. It has a shell which is in one piece, and eats plants and small animals. Gastropods live mainly among seaweeds. Pools among the rocks are good places to look for **crustaceans** such as crabs, prawns, and shrimps. Here too are sea anemones, small animals that look like plants.

▼ Some very odd creatures are to be found along the shoreline. The hermit crab has no shell of its own. Instead it moves into the shell of another animal — often a whelk. The female starfish can lay up to three million eggs. If a starfish loses an arm, it simply grows another one. The butterfish, or gunnel can stay behind when the tide has gone out. It hides in pools, under rocks and seaweed.

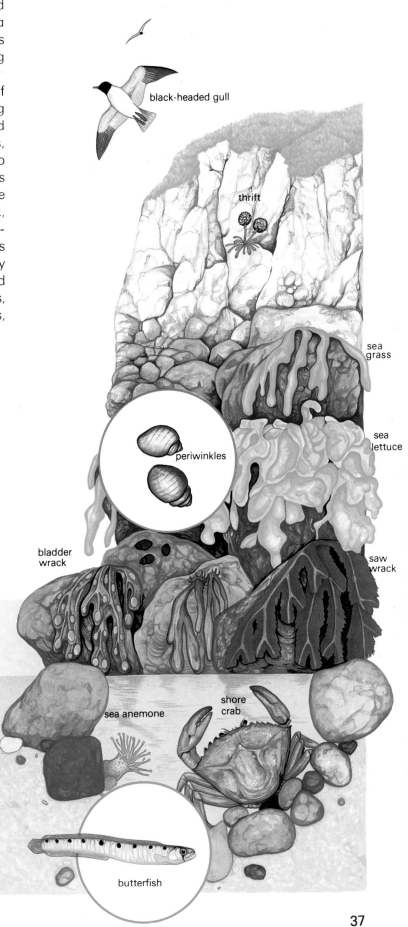

black-headed gull

thrift

sea grass

sea lettuce

periwinkles

saw wrack

bladder wrack

hermit crab

high tide

low tide

common prawn

sea urchin

razor shell

starfish

cockle

necklace shell

sea anemone

shore crab

butterfish

37

In the Sea

So much of our planet is covered with water that it looks blue from space! It was in these seas that the very first living things appeared, millions of years ago. Today the seas are still full of plant and animal life.

Surface Swimmers
The light and warmth of the sun only reach down through the water for 500 feet. Near the top of these sunny waters live millions of minute animals and plants. Together they are known as **plankton**. They drift in the ocean currents, and provide food for many kinds of fish, among them the world's largest, the whale shark. Some whales eat plankton. Other whales, seals, and dolphins feed on fish. Sea mammals, such as whales and porpoises, breathe through lungs, as we do. This means that they have to come to the surface from time to time for a breath of air.

Near land, enough light reaches the shallow seabed for plants to grow. Among them live octopuses, jellyfish, lobsters, and flatfish, such as flounders. Sponges are not plants, but animals that anchor themselves to the rocks.

Monsters of the Deep
In the dim world of the deeper waters live all kinds of strange creatures. Many of the fish here are brilliantly colored. In darker waters, many of them can make their own light. The angler fish dangles a light over its head, luring other fishes into its toothy jaws. Some of these creatures have special sight. The giant squid has the largest eyes of any living creature.

At the bottom of the deepest ocean the waters are

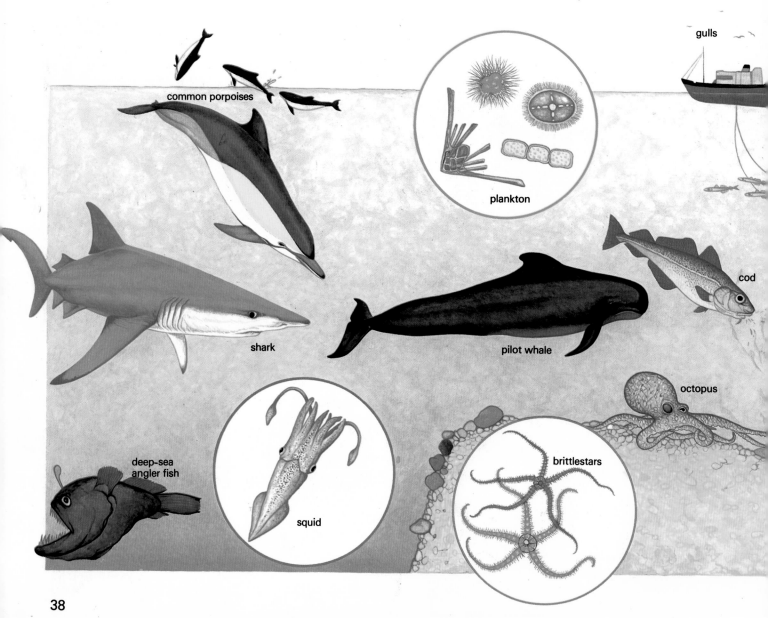

gulls

common porpoises

plankton

cod

shark

pilot whale

octopus

deep-sea angler fish

squid

brittlestars

as black as the night. Here the creatures have little color. They use hearing and their sense of smell instead of sight. All the seabed is covered with the remains of plants and animals that have sunk slowly down from the upper waters.

▶ In warm, shallow seas corals make hard cases around their soft bodies. These may build up into huge reefs. Vast shoals of tiny, brilliantly colored clown fish and butterfly fish live among the corals.

▼ This picture shows life in northern waters. The plankton and the fish that feed on it live near the surface of the sea. Among them are sprats, mackerel, and herring, which swim around in huge shoals. Seabirds, and some of the larger fish and sea-living mammals feed off them. Fish is a good source of food for us too — the trawler in the picture is catching cod in its net.

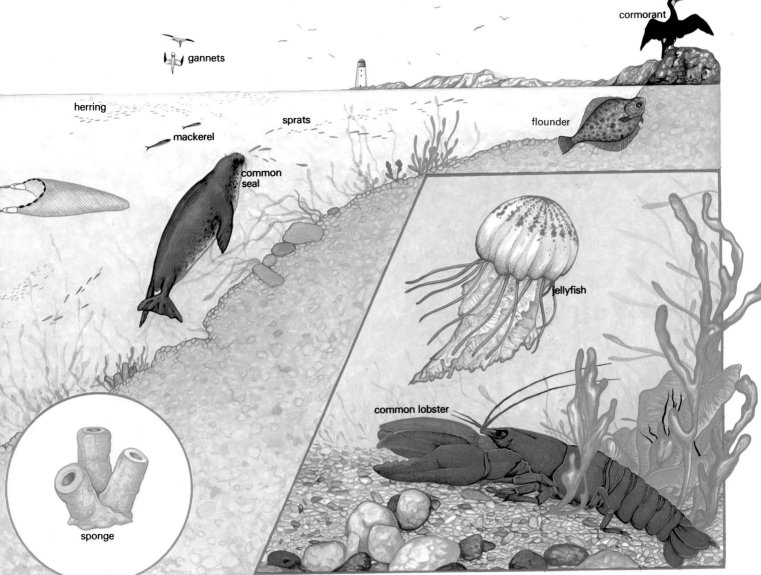

cormorant

gannets

herring

sprats

mackerel

flounder

common seal

jellyfish

common lobster

sponge

▶ The house martin builds a cup-shaped nest of mud, tucked under the eaves of buildings. You may see the heads of the nestlings peeping out of the hole near the top if you are very quiet.

▶ Common wasps chew up wood to make a sort of paper, with which they build their nests underground or in hollow trees. Sometimes wasps nest in houses, in the roof or under the floorboards.

▶ Harvest mice build round nests of grass. They are slung between the stalks of strong grasses or crops like wheat. The nest is about the size of a tennis ball.

◀ The eagle builds an untidy nest from sticks high in trees or on rocky ledges. It uses the same nest year after year, adding a few more sticks each season. An eagle's nest can be as much as 10 feet across. It is called an **eyrie**.

◀ Mammals also make nests. The squirrel builds its drey in treetop branches. It is made with twigs, leaves, moss, and bark. Sometimes it builds around an old nest.

◀ The thrush builds a cup-shaped nest in trees, bushes, and hedges. It is hidden among the leaves. The thrush often uses feathers or grasses, and lines the nest with mud.

◀ Even a fish can make a nest! The male stickleback arranges the stems of water plants into a tunnel. Here the female will lay her eggs. The male then watches over them until they hatch.

▲ Beavers are very clever builders. They chop down small trees with their sharp teeth and use them to dam a stream. Before long a pool collects behind the dam, and here the beavers build their nest or **lodge**. They pile up stones, branches, and mud in the pool, and then gnaw tunnels and living rooms in the pile. The entrance is under water, but the nest chamber is above the water level so that air can get in for them to breathe.

Homes and Young

Animals make their homes in all sorts of places. Some, such as rabbits, use their homes for protection and bringing up their young. Others, including many birds, build complicated nests and only use them in the breeding season. Insects lay their eggs in places where there will be food for the young when they hatch. Houseflies, for example, lay their eggs in rotting food.

In cold climates some animals, such as hedgehogs, tortoises, and snakes, spend the winter asleep in caves or under the ground. This winter sleep is called **hibernation**.

Many animals, such as antelope, have no homes. They wander about all through their lives. Their young are so well developed when born that they can stagger to their feet almost immediately.

All Kinds of Nests

The easiest animal homes to see are nests. Many kinds of animals build them, and birds are the experts. They use all kinds of materials, including grass, twigs, clay, and even human rubbish such as bits of polythene and candy wrappers! Some nests are small and neat, others huge and untidy. Guillemots, which breed on sea cliffs, make no nest at all. They lay a

◀ The froghopper, a tiny insect, lays its eggs on a plant stem. When the young hatches, it surrounds itself with foam to protect it from drying up.

▲ Home for the baby kangaroo is its mother's pouch. It crawls there as soon as it is born to suck its mother's milk. Even quite large kangaroos hop back into the pouch to be carried around with the herd.

pear-shaped egg straight on to a narrow rock ledge. The hare and some other animals just scrape a little hole in the ground for their young.

Burrows and Holes

Many animals live in underground burrows. Among them are rabbits, badgers, and foxes. Hedgehogs shelter in holes in or near walls. Others find shelter in hollows in trees and banks. Bats find buildings a good place in which to live and bring up their young.

▲ Swans are good parents. When the cygnets have hatched, they often clamber on to their parents' backs for a ride. The family stays together until the young are fully grown, and the male and female birds stay together for life. Many other animals carry their young around like this, clinging to their backs or even slung underneath them.

▼ Tunnels underground make safe homes for many animals. The rabbit builds a **warren** of tunnels and chambers in which to shelter from enemies and to bring up its young. These are born naked, blind, and helpless. Sometimes animals take over one another's homes; here a puffin bobs out of a rabbit burrow. Badgers and foxes both live in woods and sometimes a fox will take over part of a badger's **set** for its **earth**. Hedgehogs nest in the shelter of a crumbling wall. There they can hibernate for the winter. The adder hibernates under stones or in a burrow.

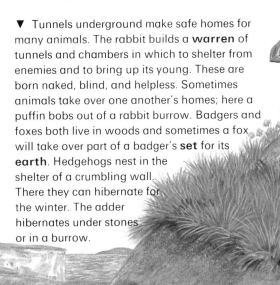

adder hibernating

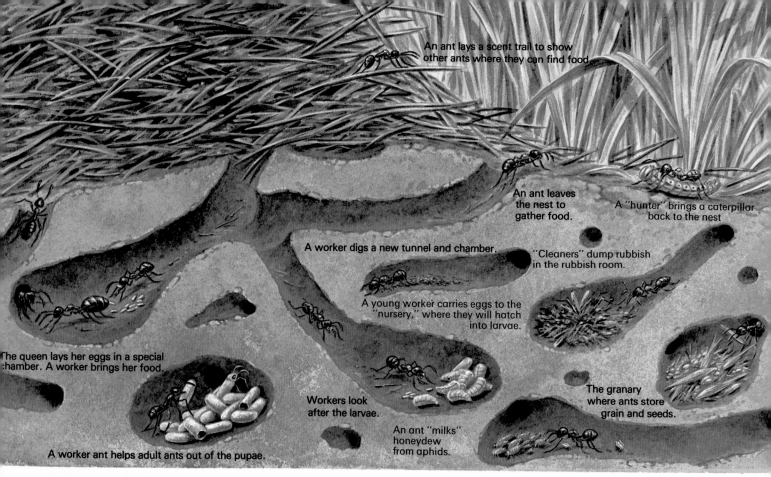

An ant lays a scent trail to show other ants where they can find food

An ant leaves the nest to gather food.

A "hunter" brings a caterpillar back to the nest

A worker digs a new tunnel and chamber.

"Cleaners" dump rubbish in the rubbish room.

A young worker carries eggs to the "nursery," where they will hatch into larvae.

The queen lays her eggs in a special chamber. A worker brings her food.

Workers look after the larvae.

The granary where ants store grain and seeds.

An ant "milks" honeydew from aphids.

A worker ant helps adult ants out of the pupae.

▲ Each ant in this nest has its own special job which helps the group — collecting food, looking after the young, building, cleaning, and fighting. Insects that live and work together like this are called **social insects.**

▼ The fierce Nile crocodile lets a little plover hop right into its mouth. The plover picks tiny parasites from the crocodile's gums. This helps both animals; the crocodile has clean gums and the plover has food. In the same way, large fish let "cleaner" fish eat the parasites living on them.

spur-winged plover

Nile crocodile

Living Together

Many animals live together, in small groups or in thousands. They do this to help find food and to protect one another. Some insects, such as ants, termites, and honeybees, are very well organized. The work is shared and each insect in the group has its own job to do, which helps the group as a whole.

Some birds, too, live in colonies of hundreds. Penguins, starlings, and gulls, for example, often gather in large, noisy crowds. But each bird has its own small patch of territory where it nests and raises its young, and it will fight off intruders. Zebra and reindeer too keep together in herds, and all the animals look out for danger and warn one another.

Animals Partners
Sometimes animals of two different kinds live together. This sort of arrangement often helps only one of the animals, for example the flea that lives in the fur of mammals and feeds on their blood. The animal that benefits is called a **parasite.** In other cases, the partnership helps both animals. The hermit crab lives inside the shell of a dead sea snail. Sometimes a sea anemone lives on the shell. The anemone gets a free ride to find food, and in return its stinging tentacles keep the crab's enemies away.

prairie
dogs

▲ A group of baboons. These live in well organized groups. The senior males, females, and their babies are guarded by the younger and less important males. These generally live on the outside of the baboon **troop**. Baboons spend a lot of time grooming one another, searching through the thick fur for parasites such as fleas. Many animals enjoy doing this and it helps to keep all the group living happily together.

▲▶ Prairie dogs live in large "towns" of many burrows. Some keep a sharp lookout for danger while others feed and play.

▶ Breeding gannets and guillemots crowd together on this rock. Different seabirds often nest crammed together in mixed colonies like this; but each has its own particular nesting area or territory. Land birds are more widely spread about, but again each pair will have a territory where it nests and feeds. It will drive away any other bird of the same kind that comes too close.

▼ Living together helps these wolves to get food. Hunting in a pack is better than hunting in ones and twos. The musk-ox live together partly for defense. When attacked, they make a circle, facing outward, protecting their young in the center.

wolves

musk-oxen

Animal Journeys

▼ Migrating birds such as these geese gather in flocks of thousands for their journeys. Geese fly by night and day; smaller, insect-eating birds travel at night and rest and feed in daytime. Birds return to the same nests each year after journeys of hundreds of miles.

Animals have two most important activities, feeding and breeding. For many of them, finding something to eat or somewhere to breed means making a journey. When this journey happens regularly, there and back each year, it is called **migration**.

Long-distance Travelers

All kinds of animals migrate — insects, fish, birds, and mammals. They often make a very long journey. Many migrants follow the sunshine. As winter comes, the cold kills off insects. The ground begins to freeze, making it difficult for many birds and land mammals to feed. So, to avoid starving to death, they move to warmer parts of the world where they are sure of finding food. The following spring they return home.

One animal that migrates to escape winter is the caribou of North America. Huge herds of caribou leave the Arctic and travel 800 miles south to the shelter of forests. Here they can feed on lichens, buds, and shoots. Monarch butterflies migrate south from Canada in the fall; some reach Mexico, a trip of over 1,700 miles. Some birds travel even farther.

Breeding Grounds

Other animals migrate to special breeding grounds. Frogs make their way to ponds for spawning; salmon leave the sea and swim up rivers to lay their eggs in fresh water; and some sea turtles travel 2,500 miles to breed on islands in the south Atlantic.

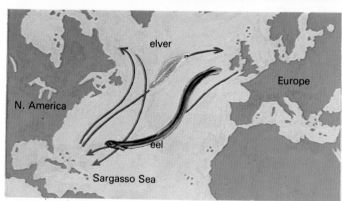

▲ European and American eels usually live in rivers, but when they are ready to breed they swim to the coast and out across the ocean to the Sargasso Sea. There they lay their eggs and die. After hatching, the young eels — elvers — swim back to the rivers. The 5,000-mile journey to Europe takes three years.

◄ This map shows the migration routes of four long-distance fliers: the white-footed goose, cuckoo, swallow, and Arctic tern. The Arctic tern travels farther than any other migrating bird. As winter approaches in the north, it leaves the Arctic and flies halfway around the world to spend summer in the Antarctic. Six months later, the tern returns to the north, making a round trip of 18,000 miles. How migrating birds find their way is a mystery. But they seem to navigate by the sun and stars and use landmarks on the ground below. It is also possible that birds are affected by the earth's magnetism, as if they had a built-in compass.

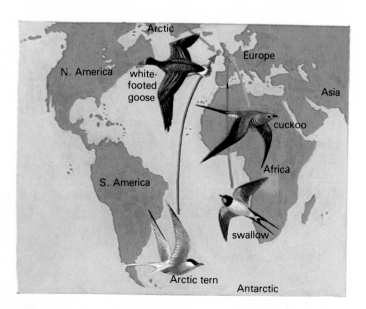

◄ The Alaskan fur seal breeds on the shores of the Pribilof islands near Alaska. The females and young then swim some 3,000 miles south to live in the warm seas off California; the males remain in the north. The following year, the mothers and children swim back.

In some cases, the outward journey is made by the adult and the journey back by its descendants. The red admiral butterfly, that comes from the Mediterranean to spend the summer in Britain, does not fly back again. But its offspring do, and when they reach the southern lands, they breed there. In turn, their offspring journey north, back to Britain.

Not all animal journeys are migrations. Some are only one way. This often happens when food supplies and weather conditions are so good that creatures breed rapidly and overcrowd their home area. Then some of them have to move away to find more food and space. When the locust population suddenly gets bigger, for example, the insects swarm together in millions and fly across the land, eating all the plants as they go. Lemmings too leave their home when there are too many of them to share the food. They move in great armies to settle elsewhere. The crossbill has a special diet of fir-cone seeds. If the cone harvest is poor the bird must leave the northern forests and fly south in search of other fir trees.

▲ By May each year the wildebeeste of the Serengeti grasslands in Africa have cropped down the grass. A million or more move slowly northeast to fresh grasslands. These last them until November. Then they go back to the Serengeti where rain has fallen and new grass has grown.

▼ The painted lady butterfly often covers thousands of miles in its migration journey. In summer, these butterflies can be found as far north as the Arctic Circle and in winter, as far south as Africa and the Near East.

KEEP A VISITORS' BOOK

notebook

pencil

If you watch the birds in your garden, you will find that some are there almost every day, but others just come in summer or winter. Make a record of these in a notebook. Write down the date when you first see them, and describe the weather. If you can, paste in a photograph. Find out from a bird guide when the visitor is likely to leave and watch specially carefully for its last appear- ance. Write down that date, too.

Next year watch to see whether the same birds arrive — and whether they come at about the same date.

Atlantic Ocean

Europe

painted lady

N. Africa

CAMOUFLAGE

stick insect

peppered moth

flounder

little tern's eggs

tiger

stoat in winter

stoat in summer

Camouflage helps many animals to look the same as their surroundings. Most use it for defense, but hunting animals such as the tiger use it to get near to their prey. Some animals change their camouflage with the seasons.

▼ Can you see the insect among the leaves? Its camouflage is almost perfect as long as it keeps quite still.

Curiosities

Animals come in all colors and shapes. Some of them seem amazing, but they are there for a purpose. Colors and shapes help animals to stay alive and raise their young in the particular places in which they live.

Helpful Coloring

The simplest way to escape an enemy is to run away, and many animals do just that. Others stay absolutely still and rely on their shapes and colors to hide them. This is known as **camouflage**, and you can see some well camouflaged animals in the pictures on the left. A few, such as the chameleon and the squid, change color to match the background as they move.

Some animals protect their bodies with spines or bony plates. Others try to confuse their attackers. Squids and octopuses squirt a cloud of inky fluid into

WEAPONS AND DEFENCE

red deer

▲ These fighting deer look fierce, but they will probably do each other little harm. They lock their antlers and struggle together; then the weaker one will move off. Fights like this happen when a young stag wants to take over the grazing area and females of another, usually older stag. Many male animals have this sort of fight but few really hurt their own kind.

coral snake

wasp

▶ These animals are all poisonous. Their bright colors say "Beware" to attackers. Some of these animals sting or bite their enemies; others are poisonous when eaten, or taste disgusting.

arrow-poison frog

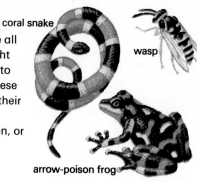

electric ray

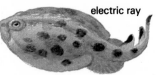

◀ The electric ray can give its attackers a nasty shock. It also uses its "sting" to stun its prey.

the water, which hides them while they swim away. The bright color of some creatures, including wasps, many moths, and small frogs, warn that they are poisonous. Some quite harmless animals look very like poisonous ones. Their enemies may think they too are dangerous, and leave them alone.

The brilliantly colored feathers of many male birds are used not to warn off enemies, but to attract a mate. The males flutter their feathers, call and strut around in front of the females. Other animals, too, use color in the breeding season. Even the tiny male stickleback develops a brilliant red patch.

Special Shapes

If we look carefully at animals, we can see how their bodies have developed to suit the conditions they live in. A few rather special ways are shown below. Often animals that have a similar way of life look alike, even though they are not related to one another. A dolphin looks much like a huge shark. Though one is a mammal and the other a fish, both have bodies adapted to live in water.

▲ This magnificent male peacock is displaying in front of a female. After the breeding season, the long feathers will fall out. The peahen, like many other female birds, does not have bright feathers. Her drab plumage protects her as she sits on her nest.

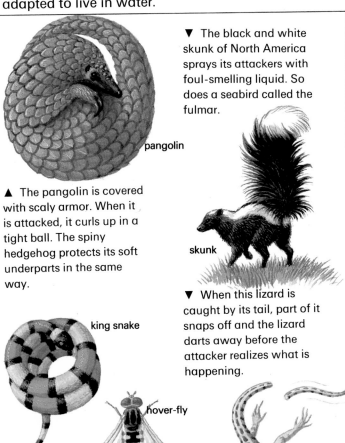

▼ The black and white skunk of North America sprays its attackers with foul-smelling liquid. So does a seabird called the fulmar.

pangolin

skunk

▲ The pangolin is covered with scaly armor. When it is attacked, it curls up in a tight ball. The spiny hedgehog protects its soft underparts in the same way.

king snake

▼ When this lizard is caught by its tail, part of it snaps off and the lizard darts away before the attacker realizes what is happening.

hover-fly

common lizard

▲ These animals are harmless. They look very like the poisonous ones on the left and so are left alone. This is called **protective mimicry**.

SPECIAL ADAPTATIONS

common long-eared bat

▼ The mole's large foot, shaped rather like a spade, helps it to dig through the soil at astonishing speed.

mole's forefoot

▲ The bat hunts at night. It sends out soundwaves that are reflected back from the insects it eats. Its huge ears help it to catch these signals.

▼ The little tarsier is a tree-living creature, active during the night. Its large eyes help it to see in the dark, and its large ears help it to hear well. It has a long tail and very long legs with which to grasp the tree, and the pads on its toes give it a good grip.

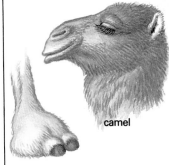

camel

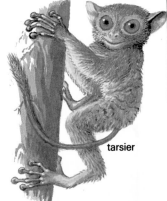

tarsier

▲ The camel has long eyelashes and slit-like nostrils which keep out sand. Its spreading feet help it walk across the soft dunes.

The Animal World at Night

As dusk falls, the animals that have been busy all day come back to their burrows, nests, or roosts and settle down to rest. Some snatch a late meal, and blackbirds give a last loud call before tucking their heads under their wings. Flowers and plants stop making food as light fades, and some close their petals and even their leaves until morning.

Animals of the Dusk

Now the nighttime creatures are waking up, and coming out of their daytime hiding places. Moths flutter through the dusk, attracted by scent produced by flowers such as the honeysuckle. The nightjar, a twilight bird, swoops down to feed on the moths; like many other animals of the dusk and dark, it has large eyes to help it see in the poor light. The shy fallow deer come out to eat grass, leaves, and berries. Rabbits nibble the grass, keeping a wary lookout for their enemies the foxes, stoats, and badgers that are setting out for their nightly hunt.

In the Dark

The damp night air brings out moisture-loving creatures such as slugs, worms and snails, woodlice, and centipedes. Large-eyed woodmice hunt them. Hedgehogs have poor sight but a keen sense of smell; they sniff noisily around for their insect food. Frogs and toads search for slugs and other prey.

In the air, moths and other insects flutter about. Bats swoop after them, using their special "radar" system to find their insect prey. Owls flap noiselessly through the air, their wings muffled with soft-edged feathers. On clear nights in spring and autumn you may hear geese or curlew calling as migrating flocks pass overhead. Sometimes you hear the sharp bark of a fox or the grunt of a badger.

Dawn Chorus

As daylight comes, the animals of the night return to their resting places. The roosting birds wake; first one, then another begins to sing until the air is noisy with their dawn chorus. Flowers unfold and leaves begin to use the light to make food. The daytime animals come out to take up their busy lives once more.

The picture on the left shows a woodland edge at dusk. The blackbird gives a last call and the thrush settles on its nighttime perch. The long-beaked woodcock flies out and a nightjar swoops, beak open, at an insect. Rabbits and deer nibble grass; the fox and stripey-headed badger set out to hunt food. In the foreground wood sorrel closes leaves and petals and a moth hovers around the honeysuckle. The nightingale warbles its song.

The middle picture shows the same scene at night. In the foreground a frog, toad, slugs, snails, and woodlice are feeding, watched by a woodmouse and a hedgehog. Bats and an owl chase after moths and other insects.

On the right, dawn is breaking. The nighttime animals are returning to the shelter of the wood; the rabbit is having an early feed. The thrush and blackbird sing.

▲ The badger comes out as night falls, and shuffles off in search of insects, grubs, snails, and worms to eat. It also feeds on roots and berries and loves honey. Badgers live in woody country, digging roomy burrows or "sets" in light soil. Go badger-watching with a grown-up; if you keep still and are lucky, you may see some playing.

oryx
oasis
camels
McQueen buzzard
addax
gemsbok
narras
fennec
monitor
locust
jerboa
hamster

▲ In the deserts of Africa, shown on this page, there are many plant-eating animals. The oryx and gemsbok are large antelopes which graze on grass, leaves, and roots. The much smaller jerboa and hamster feed on seeds. But in turn, these small creatures are prey for bustards, fennec foxes, and other flesh-eaters. Snakes, too, will kill small animals.

Kangaroos live on the hot dry plains that cover half Australia. The kangaroo is a marsupial (so is the mouse on the right) which means it carries its baby in a pouch. The kangaroo and the hopping mouse both have long, strong back legs and move around by leaping. This is easier than running on loose, dry soil.

kangaroo
marsupial mouse
hopping mouse

Deserts

Desert are harsh, dry lands. But even though no rain may fall there for many years, many plants and animals find enough water to survive.

The picture above shows a desert in Africa. On the opposite page is one in North America. The plants and animals living there look rather alike, but they are not closely related. They have developed the same sort of shapes and ways of life to suit the similar conditions.

Storing Water

Desert plants must save water to survive. Some store water from the rare occasions when it rains in thick, fleshy leaves. These have a waxy coat to prevent moisture from leaking into the air. Others have hairs on their leaves to protect them from drying winds. Many are covered with prickly spines to stop animals from feeding on them and taking their water. Desert plants have root systems that allow them to take in as much water as possible. Some have a huge network of shallow roots; others send roots to find water deep underground.

bighorn sheep

pronghorn

elf owl

saguaro cactus

prickly pear

kit fox

barrel cactus

lynx

rattlesnake

collared lizard

kangaroo rat

grasshopper

pocket mouse

▲ Many cacti grow in the deserts of North America and they all have expert ways of storing water. The saguaro cactus, which lives for hundreds of years, can hold many gallons of water in its tall, thick stem. The prickly pear, another cactus, was taken from North America to Africa and Australia and now grows in deserts there, too.

Keeping Cool

Animals, too, have special ways of surviving in the desert. They get the water they need from their food — plants and other animals — and so they can live without drinking. But they must keep cool so that they do not waste precious moisture. Small creatures avoid the heat by staying in their burrows. When night comes the desert cools down very quickly. The animals creep out of their holes to feed. When hamsters and pocket mice discover a food supply they carry some home in their cheek pouches. Larger animals lie in the shade of rocks and shrubs during the day. They too feed at night.

In many cases, animals have bodies adapted to desert life: they give off heat but keep in water. For example, the fennec fox of the Sahara and the kit fox in North America both have large ears to help them lose heat. Spiders, scorpions, snakes, and lizards all have skins that trap the moisture inside their bodies.

▼ Many desert plants live through years of drought as seeds. Then when at last it rains, they burst out into a mass of flowers and for a few days the barren land becomes a carpet of color. These flowers soon wither when the soil dries up again, but their seeds live on, waiting for the next rainstorm — which may be years away.

Grasslands

Grasslands stretch across Africa, America, and Central Asia. They are vast plains which have little rain and often poor soil, and are covered in all kinds of grass. Some grasslands are so dry that no trees can grow. Others, especially in Africa, have a rainy season and some trees and bushes can grow there. Grasslands have different names in different parts of the world, although the plants and animals found on them are very alike. The grasslands of Central Asia are called the **steppes**, those in the warm north of South America the **campos**, and those in the south **pampas**.

Savannas

In Africa the grasslands are called **savannas**. Many different animals live there. There are large numbers of plant-eating zebras, antelopes, and giraffes. Several different kinds of plant-eaters can happily share the same food. Gazelles, for example, like young grass shoots; zebras prefer tougher grass; the dik-dik eats low-growing twigs while elephants and giraffes can reach acacia leaves growing higher up.

Out in the grasslands there is little cover, so these animals have good eyesight and a keen sense of smell to detect enemies. They can run at amazing speeds to avoid danger. The flesh-eating animals that hunt them include lions, cheetahs, and wild dogs. The cheetah, running at speeds of 70 miles an hour, has little difficulty in catching prey. Lions only hunt when they are really hungry, and spend much of their time lying in the shade. Vultures, marabou storks, and other scavengers finish off the scraps. Other birds of the savannah include the ostrich and the weaver bird.

Grasslands are dry places and so they suit animals that need little or no water, especially reptiles and insects such as grasshoppers and termites. The open plains also provide no shelter from storms and for this reason many smaller creatures live in burrows.

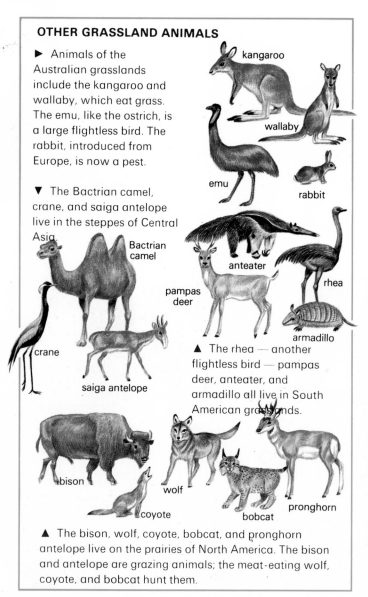

OTHER GRASSLAND ANIMALS

▶ Animals of the Australian grasslands include the kangaroo and wallaby, which eat grass. The emu, like the ostrich, is a large flightless bird. The rabbit, introduced from Europe, is now a pest.

kangaroo

wallaby

emu

rabbit

▼ The Bactrian camel, crane, and saiga antelope live in the steppes of Central Asia.

Bactrian camel

anteater

pampas deer

rhea

armadillo

crane

saiga antelope

▲ The rhea — another flightless bird — pampas deer, anteater, and armadillo all live in South American grasslands.

bison

wolf

coyote

bobcat

pronghorn

▲ The bison, wolf, coyote, bobcat, and pronghorn antelope live on the prairies of North America. The bison and antelope are grazing animals; the meat-eating wolf, coyote, and bobcat hunt them.

▼ A water hole in the African savannah. Large numbers of different animals visit it every day to drink. There are huge herds of zebras, impalas and other antelopes, and wildebeeste (only a few of each are shown in the picture). The weaver bird builds its large nest in the acacia tree, while a group of lions lies underneath, in the shade. There are many insects too; the meerkats are sitting on a termites' nest. They eat insects, such as the dung beetle, which lays its eggs in the ball of dung it has gathered.

meerkats

wildebeeste

water hole

dung-beetle

► In winter the northern grasslands of America and Central Asia are covered with snow and it is hard for animals to find enough to eat there. These bison can dig away the snow and eat the grass underneath. Once millions of them roamed the prairies but today only a few are left. They were hunted for their meat and skins, and for sport, and much of the land where they lived has been turned into farmland.

Prairies

In North America the grasslands are called **prairies** and, unlike the African savannas, have no trees at all. Several hundred years ago many creatures lived there, but today the prairies are mostly farmlands and only a few wild animals survive.

Grazing animals include bison — large, heavy creatures weighing up to a ton each, and pronghorns which can run faster than any other mammals in North America. Among the smaller plant-eaters are prairie dogs and pocket gophers; both are rodents and live in burrows. These small rodents are hunted by skunks, snakes, hawks, and eagles. But the great hunter of the prairies is the coyote which stalks by night, killing everything from gophers to pronghorns.

vulture

weaver birds

elephants

acacia tree

giraffe

ostriches

zebra

lions

impala

marabou stork

Wilson petrel

great skua

Adélie penguin

killer whale

Weddell seals

Emperor penguin

Cold Lands

The Arctic and the Antarctic, at each end of the earth, are both lonely, frozen places. But there is one big difference between them. The Arctic is mostly water, the Antarctic is mostly land. This means that different kinds of plants and animals live there.

Frozen Land

Antarctica, around the South Pole, is a vast land mass. It is covered in ice up to 15,000 feet thick and is the coldest place on earth, with temperatures as low as −110°F. No wonder Antarctica is almost lifeless. The only plants that can survive are a few lichens, mosses, and grasses that grow by the coast.

Animal life in Antarctica consists of birds and sea creatures. Penguins are the common birds there. They cannot fly; instead they use their short wings as swimming paddles. For many penguins and for flying birds such as petrels, skuas, and shags, the ice continent is just a summer nesting place. Seals and whales (including the blue whale, the largest animal alive) also come to Antarctica just for the summer. The seals breed on the beaches while the whales dive among the icebergs in the seas.

▲ On this page the picture shows wildlife in Antarctica. Only the emperor penguin lives there in winter. The male hatches the chick, resting the egg on his feet to keep it warm. Most Antarctic creatures feed on plankton and fish from the sea.

▶ Opposite is an Arctic scene. To keep warm the Arctic fox and polar bear have small ears, which lose less heat than big ones. Musk oxen grow heavy coats of long hair. The walrus has a thick layer of fat under its skin, and the polar bear even has fur on the soles of its feet.

Frozen Sea

The North Pole lies in the middle of a frozen sea which, in turn, is surrounded by land. This Arctic land, farther from its Pole, is not as cold as Antarctica and many creatures are able to live there. Some, including the caribou, are summer visitors. They move south when the long dark winter begins. Others, like the polar bear, musk ox, and lemming stay all year round, and often sleep through the winter in a burrow or snow den.

Most Arctic birds are also summer visitors. Many of them feed on the large numbers of insects that swarm over melting pools of ice in June and July. Meanwhile, as the ground thaws, thick cushions of small plants break through and very quickly burst into flower: summer lasts just six weeks, and in that short period the plants must make seeds and store up food in their roots to ensure survival through the winter.

snowy owl

musk oxen

Arctic tern

right whale

harp seals

walrus

polar bear

Arctic fox

Arctic poppy

Arctic saxifrage

lemming

moss

lemming

▼ There are about 15 species of penguins in the world and nearly all of them live in the cold waters of the Antarctic. Only two kinds of penguin, the Emperor penguin and the Adélie penguin, have their young on the Antarctic continent itself. Many other kinds, such as the rockhopper penguin shown below, live on islands in the surrounding waters. Penguins cannot fly, but are good swimmers.

macaw

king vulture

lianas

spider monkey

frog

toucan

Jungles

jaguar

Many of the world's tropical lands, around the Equator, are covered in thick jungle or rainforest. In these areas it is always hot and wet and there is little or no difference between summer and winter. Because of this, an enormous variety of flowers, bushes, and trees grows there and provides shelter and food for many different animals.

At first sight, a rainforest may seem deserted. There are several reasons for this. Many of the creatures are **nocturnal**: they spend the day in burrows or hidden among leaves and plants and then come out at night to feed. Few small plants can grow in the deep shade cast by the great trees. Most animals in the jungle spend their time not on the ground but in the trees, where they can find plenty of leaves, fruit, and insects to eat. Another reason is that the birds and butterflies that live near the ground have dull, camouflage colors; brightly colored species like toucans, parrots, hummingbirds, and the dazzling blue morpho butterfly live higher up.

In rainforests, there are very few dead leaves and decaying fruits on the ground. This is partly because there are so many insects around, especially ants and termites. In turn, these provide food for anteaters and

boa

sloth

morpho butterfly

A rainforest in South America. Jungles all over the world have the same sorts of animals living in them. Small mammals and insects live on the ground; snakes, big cats, and apes and monkeys live in the trees, while tree frogs and colorful birds live in the treetops.

orchids

tapir

cabybara

peccary

armadillo

The tropical rainforest has three main layers. Some giant trees may grow as much as 200 feet high. They stand out from the tops of other trees, which make a dense canopy of leaves about 100 feet above the ground.

Little light can get through the dense canopy. Only a few shrubs can grow beneath it, and some ferns, mosses, and fungi sprout from the forest floor. Each layer of the forest has its own special plant and animal life.

other animals with insect diets. Any plant remains rot quickly away in the damp heat.

Life in the Trees

Most jungle mammals are specially adapted to life in the trees: they have grasping hands and feet or strong tails to help them. Monkeys are good examples; so are sloths, which spend nearly all their time hanging from branches and can hardly move if they are on the ground. Even jungle hunters, like the jaguar in South America and the leopard in Africa and Asia, are very good climbers. They hide in trees, ready to pounce on their prey. Killer snakes, such as boas and pythons, also hide among branches waiting to seize a bird or mammal and squeeze it to death. The climate is so damp that tree frogs can live and breed in the jungle. Some even lay their eggs in pools of water caught in the leaves.

Tropical rainforests contain a great number of different kinds of trees. Some of these, such as mahogany, ebony, and teak, produce valuable timber. Many other plant groups, too, grow in the jungle. Two of the most typical are lianas and orchids. Lianas are climbing plants with their roots in the forest floor. They use other trees as supports while they twine upward to the top. Orchids are exotic flowers and often grow on tree branches, taking in moisture from the air through exposed roots.

▶ Once tigers like this were common in the jungles of Southeast Asia. Now there are only a few left. Many have been shot, and the jungles in which they live are being cut down.

OTHER JUNGLE ANIMALS

gorilla
guenon monkey
hornbill
okapi
bush pig

These animals are all found in the jungles of Africa. The gorilla is the largest of the apes; like the chimpanzee, it now lives only in a few areas. The bush pig and the okapi hunt on the forest floor. The hornbill's long bill can reach through thick leaves to find the fruit it eats.

parakeet
wild pig
orangutan
muntjac deer

These animals, which live in the Asian jungles, are very like other jungle animals although they are not close relations. The orangutan is an ape, living in trees. The wild pig and muntjac deer live on the ground. The parakeet, like other birds of tropical forests, has brilliantly colored feathers.

Look After Wildlife

Today there are more people living on earth than ever before. This means that they take up more room, and more room for people means less room for wildlife — plants and animals — to live in. As a result, many plants and animals are becoming scarce. Some have disappeared altogether.

For a long time, people did not realize that this was happening. They killed certain animals for sport and for meat until there were none left. They cut down huge forests for timber without planting new ones, and plowed up meadows and hillsides to grow food on. Smoke from their houses and factories carried many harmful substances into the air, which

◄ Tree-felling in the rainforests of Guyana in South America. So many trees are being felled and not replaced that the forests are shrinking quickly. Naturalists are afraid that not only will the habitats of animals be destroyed, but the climate of that part of the world may be altered.

◄▼ Planting even one tree helps! This boy is planting a tree in a wildlife park which is being made on wasteland in the city of Liverpool, England.

▼ The giant panda lives in only one part of the world, in the mountains of western China. It eats bamboo shoots. There are now very few pandas left in the wild. Scientists are hoping to breed from those kept in zoos. Some very rare animals have been bred so successfully in zoos that they can be reintroduced into the wild again.

were brought back to earth by fog and rain. Other harmful waste went into rivers, killing the plants and animals that lived there. Damaging our earth with waste in this way is called **pollution**. Unfortunately killing, destruction, and pollution still go on today. But now many people are working hard to see that wildlife is harmed as little as possible. This is called **conservation**.

How Can We Help?

Everyone can help in conservation. Governments help by making laws to stop pollution, and ordinary people can help in many ways too. On the left is the Country Code. If you follow this, you will be able to enjoy the countryside without harming the wildlife there. And remember only to pick very common wildflowers, and be very careful not to damage the plants. Never look for birds' nests in the breeding season. You may frighten the parent birds away so that the eggs cannot hatch or young may starve to death.

On page 25 you can discover some ways in which you can make a garden a good place for wildlife. In many towns and cities, groups of people interested in conservation are turning wasteland into wildlife parks and gardens in the same sort of way. Other groups are clearing rubbish out of ponds and rivers, so that plants and animals can live there.

Leaving land alone does not always make it a good place for wildlife. Often it gets overgrown with the sort of plants that make a poor home for animal life. Conservationists can help by clearing away this sort of scrubby growth.

▲ You do not have to live in the country to be a bird watcher! These members of a young ornithologists' club are looking at birds on an area of wasteland. Binoculars are a great help; they make it easy to watch birds without disturbing them.

▼ These children are taking samples of the life in an upland stream. Many streams like this are becoming so acid from pollution that fewer and fewer plants or animals can live in them.

SOME RARE AND ENDANGERED ANIMALS	
ANIMAL	**DISTRIBUTION**
Columbian white-tailed deer	Northwestern United States
Gray wolf	North America
Red kangaroo	Australia
Polar bear	Arctic regions
Giant panda	Tibet
Atlantic walrus	Northwestern Atlantic and Arctic Ocean
Black rhinoceros	Africa
Asiatic buffalo	Warmer countries of Asia
California gray whale	North Pacific
Bald eagle	North America
Peregrine falcon	Found in many parts of the world
Fin whale	Found in all oceans
West Indian manatee	West Indies and Central Asia
Leopard	Southern Asia and Africa
Ross seal	Antarctica
Pygmy hippopotamus	Liberia in Africa
California condor	Western United States
Mexican duck	Rio Grande Valley in Mexico
Whooping crane	North America
Desert tortoise	Western United States
Nilotic crocodile	Africa
Green turtle	Found in warm seas

Quiz

Can you find the answers to these questions and puzzles? The page numbers in brackets tell you where to look in the book. When you have finished, turn to page 62 to see if you are right.

The Animal Kingdom (4—13)

1 In each list, which name is the odd one out? And why?
   a crab, snail, turtle, beetle
   b frog, eel, toad, newt
   c kiwi, emu, ostrich, puffin
   d whale, seal, shark, dolphin
   e fox, giraffe, deer, zebra

2 Here are two young animals. What are their names and what do they grow into?

a

b

3 Choose the righr answers to the following questions
   a How many kinds of fish are alive today? (45,000/30,000/20,000)
   b About how many feathers does a small bird have? (90/400/2,000)
   c Which is the largest living animal? (elephant/blue whale/polar bear)
   d What are mammals with pouches called? (primates/marsupials/reptiles)

4 Are these statements true or false?
   a Fish breathe through gills
   b Reptiles are warm-blooded
   c Human beings are primates
   d Birds have hollow bones

5 Here are the names of five birds and (right) pictures of their heads. Can you match them up correctly? (swallow/mallard/curlew/woodpecker/buzzard)

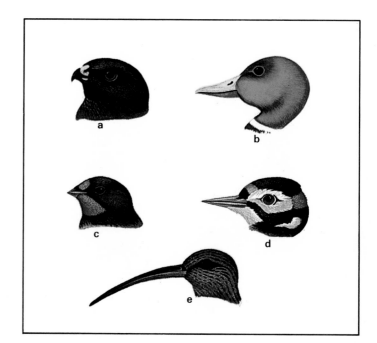

a

b

c

d

e

The Plant Kingdom (14—23)

a

b

c

d

e

1 What green chemical is found in plants?
2 What are the smallest plants?
3 Two plant groups produce seeds. What are they called?
4 Which trees keep their leaves in winter?
5 Where does moss usually grow?
6 Which conifer is deciduous?
7 What do bees and other insects carry from one flower to another?
8 What is the fruit of an oak tree called?
9 On the right are leaves and fruits of five common trees. Can you name them? Which ones are broad-leaved? Which are deciduous?
10 Are these statements true or false?
   a Shrubs have several woody stems
   b A mushroom is a fungus
   c Annual plants live for many years
   d Linen is made from hemp

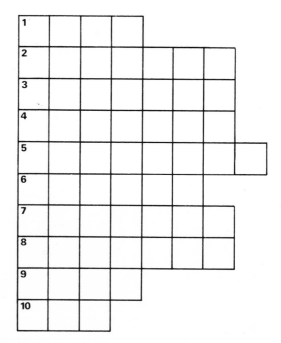

1						
2						
3						
4						
5						
6						
7						
8						
9						
10						

11 This puzzle is about the plants we use. Read the clues and fill in your answers. The first letters of the answers make up another word: the name of a plant used to flavor candies

clues:
1 Hats are made from the leaves of this tree
2 Stretchy material made of rubber
3 Common herb
4 These flowers produce opium
5 These come from deadly nightshade
6 Used for thatching
7 Made from coconut fibers
8 Powders to get rid of these are made from pyrethrum
9 Can be eaten raw or roasted
10 Its leaves make a drink

Animal Habitats (24—39)

1. Which garden flowers are favorites with bees? With butterflies?
2. Name two birds that nest on the ground
3. Which flowers grow on chalky hillsides?
4. Some animals sleep right through the winter. What is their long sleep called?
5. Name two moorland plants that eat insects
6. How many eggs can a female starfish lay?
7. What tiny animals build up into huge reefs?
8. What is the name for the millions of minute animals and plants that live near the ocean's surface?
9. Which living creature has the largest eyes?
10. Which bird can spot prey from a distance of a mile?
11. Are these statements true or false?
    a The tree creeper eats berries.
    b The mountain hare has a white coat for winter.
    c Oystercatchers only eat oysters.
    d Bats fly to warmer countries in winter.
12. These creatures all live in or near freshwater. But the letters have been jumbled up. Can you sort them out? To help you, the first letter of each name is underlined.
    TOCO GRFO
    RHIGIKNFSE TOTRE
    KEIP NOGYLFARD
    MLADRLA TEAWR LOVE
    BEERG PIDREP

 a
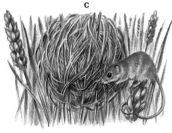 b
c

Animal Habitats (40—49)

1. Can you name the nest-builders on the right?
2. Which animals do these homes belong to?
   a set
   b earth
   c warren
   d lodge
   e drey
   f eyrie
3. Which bird lives on fir-cone seeds?
4. Which bird makes the longest migration journey?
5. Which is a young eel called?
6. Which butterfly migrates from the Arctic to Africa?
7. Which North American animal sprays attackers with a foul-smelling liquid?
8. How do hedgehogs find their food?
9. Why does the nightjar have large eyes?
10. Which animals do these feet belong to? What are they specially good for?

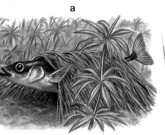

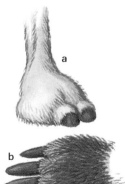
a
b

Around the World (50—57)

1. In each list, which word is the odd one out? And why?
   a polar bear, penguin, arctic fox, musk ox
   b zebra, giraffe, kangaroo, elephant
   c tiger, jaguar, leopard, cheetah
   d mahogany, ebony, acacia, teak
   e savannas, pampas, steppes, jungle
2. What kind of animals are the oryx and gemsbok?
3. Where does the fennec fox live? And the kit fox?
4. Which is the fastest mammal in North America?
5. When does the coyote hunt?
6. What are penguin colonies called?
7. How do boas and pythons kill their prey?
8. Where does the saguaro cactus store water?
9. Name two mammals that eat acacia leaves.
10. What kind of camel has two humps?
11. Choose the right answers to the following questions.
    a How fast does the cheetah run? (105/50/70 mph)
    b What is the winter temperature in Antarctica? ($-65°F/-110°F/-5°F$)
    c How high are the tallest trees in the jungle (200/260/320 feet)
    d About how many kinds of penguins are there (8/15/30)

QUIZ ANSWERS

Animal Kingdom

1. **a** turtle (vertebrate); the others are invertebrates
   b eel (fish); the others are amphibians
   c puffin; the other birds cannot fly
   d shark (fish); the other sea animals are mammals
   e fox (meat-eater); the others eat plants
2. **a** tadpole, frog
   b caterpillar, butterfly
3. **a** 30,000
   b 2,000
   c blue whale
   d marsupials
4. **a** true
   b false
   c true
   d true
5. **a** buzzard
   b mallard
   c swallow
   d woodpecker
   e curlew

Plant Kingdsom

1. chlorophyll
2. algae

3. angiosperms and gymnosperms
4. evergreens
5. in damp places
6. larch
7. pollen
8. acorn
9. **a** holly
   b beech
   c horse chestnut
   d yew
   e oak
   all are broadleaved except the yew; oak, beech, and horse chestnut are deciduous
10. **a** true
    b true
    c false
    d false
11. (in order) palm, elastic, parsley, poppies, eyedrops, rushes, matting, insects, nuts, tea; peppermint

Animal Habitats

1. hollyhocks; buddleia
2. skylark; lapwing
3. orchids
4. hibernation
5. sundew; butterwort
6. up to 3 million

7. coral
8. plankton
9. giant squid
10. golden eagle
11. **a** false
    b true
    c false
    d false
12. coot, frog, kingfisher, otter, pike, dragonfly, mallard, water vole, grebe, dipper

Animal Habitats

1. **a** stickleback
   b wasp
   c harvest mouse
2. **a** badger
   b fox
   c rabbit
   d beaver
   e squirrel
   f eagle
3. crossbill
4. Arctic tern
5. elver
6. Painted Lady
7. skunk
8. by smell
9. to see in the dark
10. **a** camel, walking on sand
    b mole, digging

Around the World

1. **a** penguin (Antarctic); the others are northern animals
   b kangaroo (Australia); the others belong to Africa. The kangaroo is also a marsupial
   c jaguar (South America); the others are found in Asia and (except the tiger) in Africa
   d acacia (savanna tree); the others grow in tropical rainforests
   e jungle; the others are all grasslands
2. antelopes
3. Sahara; North America
4. pronghorn
5. at night
6. rookeries
7. by squeezing
8. in its stem
9. elephant and giraffe
10. Bactrian
11. **a** 70 mph
    b −110°F
    c 15

Index

Figures in *Italics (sloping type)* indicate an illustration

ACKNOWLEDGEMENTS

Page 4 M. Walker/NHPA; 6 Heather Angel; 7 Bruce Coleman; 9 S. Dalton/NHPA; 10 E. A. Janes/NHPA; 16, 21, 23 Heather Angel; 30 R. B. Balharry/NHPA; 35 Heather Angel; 39 Zefa; 41 Heather Angel; 43 top Zefa, bottom Heather Angel; 45 Pearson/Biofotos; 46, 47 Pat Morris; 49 G. Kinns/Biofotos; 51 Heather Angel; 53 J. Foott/Bruce Coleman; 55 N. P. Harris/Nature Photographers; 57 Brian Hawkes; 58 top left B. Rogers/Biofotos, bottom left Conservation Volunteers, bottom right Pat Morris; 59 top Young Ornithologists' Club, bottom Heather Angel.

Picture Research: Penny J. Warn.